A Mother's Worst Fear Becomes a Healing Journey

Melanie Barton Bragg

DocUmeant *Publishing*
244 5th Avenue
Suite G-200
NY, NY 10001
646-233-4366
www.DocUmeantPublishing.com

Published by
DocUmeant Publishing
244 5th Avenue, Suite G-200
NY, NY 10001
646-233-4366

Limit of Liability and Disclaimer of Warranty: The publisher has used its best efforts in preparing this book and the information provided herein is provided "as is".

Medical Liability Disclaimer: This book is sold with the understanding that the publisher and the author are not engaged in rendering any legal, medical, or any other professional services. If expert assistance is required, the services of a competent professional should be sought.

Permission should be addressed in writing to:
    publisher@DocUmeantPublishing.com

Editor: Saundra Kelley

Asst. Editor: Philip S. Marks

Cover Design by Patti Knoles, www.virtualgraphicartsdepartment.com

Layout by DocUmeant Designs, www.DocUmeantDesigns.com

Library of Congress Cataloging-in-Publication Data

Names: Barton Bragg, Melanie, author.
Title: A mother's worst fear becomes a journey of healing / Melanie Barton
    Bragg.
Description: New York : DocUmeant Publishing, [2022] | Summary: "A Mother's
    Worst Fear Becomes a Journey of Healing brings a perspective that most
    school employees do not see from the surface. Mental health challenges
    that students and families deal with are more than meets the eye. It brings
    awareness to the real need for attention to mental health in schools. This
    book would be a beneficial read for current and aspiring school leadership.
    Counselors and school psychologists could gain from the medical as well
    as family oriented mental health concerns brought to light in this book.
    School safety and threat assessment teams could benefit from the case study
    of what could have been done to mitigate the tragedy when the student first
    started to show signs of aggression.
School administration could learn what "restorative justice" is and how to
    implement it into less severe situations such as bullying and fights. All in
    all, this book would be an asset to any school related employee's library
    and should be must read in an Education Leadership program for aspiring
    school administrators"-- Provided by publisher.
Identifiers: LCCN 2022002011 | ISBN 9781950075744 (Paperback) | ISBN
    9781950075751 (ePub)
Subjects: LCSH: Students--Mental health--United States. | Students--Mental
    health services--United States. | School improvement programs--United
    States. | School violence--United States--Prevention. | Schools--United
    States--Safety measures. | Restorative justice--United States.
Classification: LCC LB3430 .B37 2022 | DDC 371.7/13--dc23/eng/20220310
LC record available at https://lccn.loc.gov/2022002011

This book is dedicated to the memory of Agnes Furey, a Restorative Justice Advocate, who died as this book neared completion.

Contents

Preface

MY PURPOSE IN writing this book is to help people consider the many factors that can lead to the commission of a crime. If the victim and perpetrator can dialogue with professional facilitation without re-traumatization about these factors, healing may result, and recidivism be averted.

As a psychotherapist, I practiced Restorative Justice throughout my forty-year career without knowing there was such a term. It wasn't until the fall of 2017, when I met Agnes Furey, a powerful force in the local and National Justice Tallahassee community, that I began to understand the value of the practice. Afterward, I read the book she co-wrote with Leonard Scovens.

Their book, *Wildflowers in the Median: A Restorative Journey into Healing*, focuses on rehabilitating offenders through reconciliation with the victim and community at large.

This practice can break down the wall that separates the injured from the accused and prevents impaired mental health for both the victim and the perpetrator. My involvement in cases has had such a profound impact on my life, both positive and negative; I wanted to write a story so readers could witness how Restorative Justice can work. To help me better understand the perspective of the victim's family, I read Kate Grosmaire's book *Forgiving my Daughter's Killer* and Mattie Carroll Mullins' story *Judy*.

Early in my career, I learned my clients involved in the court system, whether they are the offender or the victim, are often unjustly treated. It became evident to me in 1979 when I served as the founding executive director at the Cumbee Center (Coalition to Assist Abused Persons) in Aiken, South Carolina. At that time, the established legal system, believing victims always returned to their abusers after an incident, failed to see how intervention could work. So, to help women escape the cycle of abuse, this agency developed services to address these issues. These programs now include mindfulness training, cognitive behavioral therapy, trauma-focused cognitive behavioral therapy, cognitive processing therapy, Eye Movement Desensitization and Reprocessing Therapy, Thera-play, and Sand Tray Play. These methods address the trauma and help the victims understand how and why they are attracted to an abuser, usually related to previous trauma.

Unfortunately, the Duluth Model used for mandated counseling for batterers only shames the person and does not address the fact that these people are usually victims of violence themselves from a very young age. Addressing their victimization will help end the cycle of abuse.

Later as a social work intern in a South Carolina male youth correctional institution, I discovered therapy was not a high priority at that facility. Most of the incarcerated young men could not read and or had learning disabilities, suffered from extreme child neglect and abuse, and had no viable support network. They needed long-term intensive psychotherapy, but according to their sentence, all that was mandated was eight sessions that did not begin until two months before release. Unfortunately, clients often missed their weekly appointments because of an extra headcount beyond the required daily five due to an inmate not being in their assigned location.

When the client was finally released to attend the session, the allotted timeslot had ended. That meant one less mandated session to help prevent recidivism by addressing their trauma.

Later, as a Pre-trial Intervention Program counselor, I approached the director on behalf of a few of my clients who were unfairly treated. They either lacked the mental capacity to understand the charges levied against them, had no means to pay for restitution or transportation to get to their sessions, or were targeted because of race. My attempts to have these requirements lessened or altered proved futile. The justice system made no allowances for these situations and seemed to punish them more harshly because they could not speak for themselves.

Since opening my practice in 1985, I have had more latitude to effect real change in my clients' treatment in the legal system. I act as a mental health advocate for my clients when their attorney and the judge listen to my input. As a result, satisfied clients and attorneys refer others to me. When there is enough evidence of how this process can help both the victim(s) and perpetrator(s) perhaps it will begin to turn the tide in changing the procedures in how all people are treated.

Before either a scheduled in-person or virtual meeting with a client's attorney, I prepare a letter detailing my client's diagnosis and treatment summary. I review it with the client for accuracy, getting them to sign a release permitting me to share it with their attorney. If my client is the victim, I document how the crime has negatively impacted their life. If they are the accused, I outline how their life circumstances have contributed to their arrest and provide documentation of how they are now exhibiting healthier behaviors. Finally, if incarceration is inevitable, we request continued consistent and timely mental health/ substance abuse/anger management treatment.

Prior to appearing in court for the sentencing hearing, I prep the traumatized victims on court etiquette and the proper way to answer questions from the bench. Victims need to describe how the crime impacted their lives and persuade the court that the perpetrator belongs in an appropriate facility. In the process of pleading their request to be granted, the victim may ask for the prison placement to be one that can provide adequate physical and mental health/substance abuse/anger management treatment, so no one else becomes a victim.

In my four decades of experience working with offenders and victims, I have found that punishment without the benefit of treatment increases recidivism and victimizes the inmate.

This type of request is an example of Restorative Justice at work, a research-supported method that can lessen the negative impact on everyone involved. For this process to work, the defense attorney, prosecutor, and judge must be open to the idea. Presenting research to support the victim's request for the offender to have treatment may help sway the judge's decision.

Counseling parents, even minutes after learning their child died due to murder, all the way through the court process and the sentencing, there is always an unfinished piece to reckon with—the eventual parole. It weighs heavy on people's minds like a dark specter on the horizon, even if it is unconscious. It has a long-term effect on everyone's physical and mental health, including mine, their therapist. My client's stress of having no say in what happens to the perpetrator until the sentencing hearing or parole is an elongated nightmare.

I have counseled families who had to decide if the person who killed or raped their child should be released or remain incarcerated. I have witnessed victims who couldn't find closure until they could provide personal input in the outcome.

Further, because I have treated families where one member, due to a psychotic episode, a rage blackout, or a drunken stupor, killed one of their loved ones, I now teach anger management and listening skills to all my clients.

The following story is a fictionalized compilation of my own personal and professional experiences with Restorative Justice. My goal is to guide both victims and perpetrators to find healing and resolution through a better understanding of the process.

Names, characters, businesses, places, events, and incidents are either products of my imagination or used in a fictitious manner. Any resemblance to actual persons living or dead or actual events is coincidental.

Acknowledgments

FIRST, I WOULD like to thank my critique group consisting of Patty Daniels, Gwen Williams, Pat Stanford, and Nancy Redfern-Vance, who provided ongoing editing suggestions. My ever-supportive sister, Robin Pearson, offered suggestions for the cover art. When she and I put our heads together, great things come forth. Captain K.C. Strickland, retired law enforcement officer, read the book for accuracy of details relating to handling police matters. Chief Finance Counsel attorney Miriam Wilkinson examined the document for proper legal terms and procedures. Kevin Helms, FSUS Dean of Students, reviewed the book for accuracy about how schools handle tragedies. Erik Simmons, retired Institutional Security Specialist from Chattahoochee State Hospital, reviewed the draft for accuracy concerning the methods used to handle different scenarios with forensic patients. Connie Stoutamire of Keep It Simple Photography, with her experienced eye, snapped the author's photo. Saundra Kelley, an award-winning author, was my editor who helped me express myself with attention-grabbing wording and phrasing. Lastly, kudos to my formatter, Ginger Marks, and cover artist, Patti Knoles, who pulled it all together. I thank you all for your contribution.

Fear Becomes Reality

WHEN SANDY JONES' Fitbit alarm sounded, she jumped; it was 10:45 am, time to take her Lamictal tablet. Though it had been two years since her last manic episode, she dutifully swallowed the tablet with a swig of lukewarm macchiato. Before turning back to her computer, she checked the fitness app again and exhaled loudly: I've only taken 1,500 steps so far today!

Staring in dismay at her computer screen and notes spread out on the desk, she sighed heavily, muttering under her breath, "my budget proposal is due in three hours, and here I am, still crunching the numbers! I'm always behind on Mondays. I've got to step it up."

Hearing her loud sigh, Sandy's co-worker Meg peeked over the top of their shared cubicle divider. "Hey girl," she said, "were you talking to me? If so, speak up."

Looking up in surprise, Sandy said, "I'm sorry, Meg, I didn't know you could hear me. I was giving myself a little pep talk. It did me about as much good as this cold cup of coffee."

Before she could say more, her cellphone rang. "Sorry Meg, I gotta get this. It's Garrison's school. I hope he's not sick again; I can't afford to take any more time off."

"Okay. Catch ya, later," Meg said, disappearing behind her cubicle again.

Inserting her earbud, Sandy answered the phone, "Hello, this is Sandy Jones."

"Ms. Jones, this is Tom Edwards, principal at Greenwood Middle School. Can you speak privately?"

Sandy felt her chest squeeze at the tone in his voice. *Something is wrong. I can tell it.* "Is Garrison sick again?" Finally, when he remained silent for a second too long, she spoke. "Please, Mr. Edwards, tell me why you're calling."

"Um, Ma'am, you haven't read the school Twitter post we put up about ten minutes ago, have you?"

"No, I haven't; I'm at work. What have I missed? Please don't tell me Garrison is sick again!"

"No, ma'am, that's not why I am calling, but there has been an incident at the school. Unfortunately, I can't tell you anything more right now. You will need to go to Metro emergency room for more details. "

Interrupting the principal, Sandy screamed into the phone. "What are you trying to tell me? Has my son been hurt? Is he all right?"

Overhearing the conversation, Meg was already on her feet when Sandy cried out. She leaned over the top of the cubicle, waiting with bated breath; she feared whatever was happening could throw her friend into another mental health crisis.

Principal Edwards responded to her stress in a calm voice, "Ma'am, I can't tell you anything more right now. You'll have to go to the ER for more information."

"Mr. Edwards, you must tell me something," Sandy demanded.

Taking a deep breath, he paused before answering, "One of our students wielded a knife in the classroom, and your son is one of the wounded. An ambulance transported Garrison and the other injured students to the ER ten minutes ago. I am sorry I can't say more. I have other parents to call. Just go to the Metro ER, and someone there will provide you with more details."

When the line went dead, Sandy's knees began shaking. She mumbled, "Garrison's been hurt. The principal says I must go to the ER."

Meg snatched her handbag, without a second thought, then rushed around the divider to Sandy's cubicle. Taking charge of the situation, she grabbed Sandy's purse with her keys, took the cellphone from her hand, and guided her to the receptionist at the front desk. She told the woman where they were going then led Sandy to the car.

Fortunately, the Metro ER was only three blocks away from their office building, and traffic was light that time of day. But all the way there, Sandy repeated, "Dear God please let Garrison be okay."

Meg pulled into the parking lot, then stopped at the emergency entrance. Turning to Sandy, she said, "We have to get you inside. Will you be okay if I drop you off here? I need to find a parking space."

When her friend failed to respond, Meg walked around to the passenger side door and gently pulled Sandy up and out of the car. At the ER reception desk, they stood waiting for what seemed like an eternity for the receptionist to end a personal phone call. Impatient and concerned for Sandy, Meg read the receptionist's nametag and demanded, "Janice, where are they?"

Without lifting her eyes from the cellphone, the receptionist replied, "who are 'they' and who are you?"

"The 'they' are parents of the injured Greenwood Middle School students. I'm Meg, and this is Sandy Jones, the mother of Garrison Jones, one of those students. Principal Edwards instructed her to come here. Now, can you help us?"

At this news, Janice was able to pry her eyes from her phone. She found the newly updated patient roster and then located Garrison's name. Pointing to the right she said, "The parents are meeting over there in the conference room."

Taking Sandy by the hand, Meg turned to lead her to the conference room, but she resisted.

"I can't go in there, Meg. What if Garrison's dead? I can't stand the thought of losing him."

Meg was trying to figure out what to do next when someone tapped her on the shoulder. She turned to see it was a Metro City policeman.

"Ma'am is that your car out there?" he said. When she nodded, he added, "It's blocking the entrance, where an ambulance needs to unload. I need you to move it now, please."

Apologizing, Meg, seeing his name badge, added, "Officer Patterson, my friend was just told by her son's principal to come here because of an incident at the Greenwood Middle School. I'm trying to get her into the conference room. Can you help us?"

Officer Patterson's face clearly showed his compassion when he responded. "I understand. If you move your car, I'll escort your friend into the conference room."

Even with the kind officer at her side, Sandy froze at the door. She was desperately afraid to cross the threshold. *This is my worst nightmare.* She told herself, *if I don't go in it won't be real. I will wake up, and everything will be okay.* She knew that wasn't true when the officer spoke to her again.

Speaking gently, he said, "Ma'am, you'll be all right. Go on in."

Standing in the open doorway next to the reluctant Sandy, Officer Patterson surveyed the room of dazed, silent parents. Eyeing the chaplain next to the coffee counter, he beckoned him over.

"Chaplain Curtis, this is one of the parents of the injured kids. I'm sorry Ma'am, I didn't get your name."

"Sandy Jones, but please just call me Sandy," she said in a barely audible whisper inching into the room. The torturous thought ran in the back of her mind: *If my boy is dead does that mean I am no longer a mother?*

Breaking into her thoughts, the chaplain turned to her and asked, "I'm sorry we have to meet under these circumstances, Sandy. Can I pour you a cup of coffee?" holding up the carafe.

"Uh, coffee, no thanks. I had a cup at the office," but inside, she was thinking, I will never have a macchiato again. It will always remind me of this horrible day.

When Meg entered the conference room to look for Sandy, the chaplain approached her. Sandy spoke up before he could say a word, "she's with me," pointing Meg to the empty chair beside hers.

Sitting next to Sandy, Meg leaned over to ask, "How are you doing?"

Uncharacteristically silent, Sandy squeezed Meg's hand in response, but it was clear she had other things on her mind. Then as though snapping out of a trance Sandy stood and motioned to Officer Patterson to follow her out of the room.

On full alert, Meg watched Sandy's behavior like a mother hen, her own anxiety rising. What was her friend up to?

"Officer, I demand to know what happened at the school and who was hurt," Sandy said, wringing her hands, trembling.

The officer, who was there to provide information to the parents, cleared his throat before speaking. "I'm sorry, ma'am, I haven't received the victim status report from my commanding officer. When I get that, I will give you an update. I can tell you our paramedics transported the injured here, and the other officers are still at the school interviewing witnesses."

When he paused, Sandy saw tears in his eyes.

Resuming the conversation, he said, "Frankly, I'm just as nervous as you—my niece is one of the injured students."

The look on his face broke through Sandy's rising anxiety. She hugged him in compassion and thanked him. When they returned to the conference room, Sandy was more herself than when she left. Meg noticed the difference immediately and sighed with relief. All the parents looked up with questioning eyes, but Sandy shrugged her shoulders and sat down next to Meg again, grasping her friend's hand.

A ticking wall clock was the only sound in the room. Tic . . . tic . . .tic . . . Finally, chaplain Curtis quietly asked, "Would anyone like to pray?"

Mr. Dawson, the brown-skinned balding dad who was Sandy and Garrison's neighbor, stared at him with piercing eyes, "my God, just what do you think we've been doing here, Chaplain? Playing tiddlywinks?"

Taken aback, the chaplain responded, "Sorry, sir. I meant no disrespect. It's just that many people, religious or not, appreciate prayer in times of trauma and uncertainty."

Then red-headed Maureen Spencer turned to Chaplain Curtis and said, "I don't believe in God, so why should I pray? If there was a God, I doubt He would have allowed this 'incident' to happen to our children."

Chaplain Curtis replied gently to the distraught mom, "Okay, I will not debate that point with you, but if anyone wants to talk or to pray, I'm here for you."

Feeling the tension rise in her gut again, Sandy stared at the sad, anxious faces around her and knew she had to do something or burst. "So, when are we going to get some answers, folks? I checked the school website just now, and all it says is the building is on lockdown, and EMS transported injured individuals to Metro. We've been here for more than an hour with no news at all!"

Fortunately, Officer Patterson's phone rang just then. He darted out of the room to answer it, and on his return, the chaplain asked him, "Officer, can you tell us anything? These people need some answers."

Patterson was about to speak when Principal Edwards entered the room, followed by the school nurse, two guidance counselors, and the school basketball coach, who was also a bi-vocational preacher.

Sandy felt her heart constrict in response seeing their solemn expressions, the principal's dropping shoulders, and the new worry lines etched on his face. Did their appearance mean that a mother's worst possible fear was happening?

Without warning, long-submerged memories flooded her mind: on a crisp October morning two years ago, she had just poured her first cup of coffee and was about to wake her son Garrison for school when the doorbell rang. Upon opening the door, she gasped as an Army Field

Grade Officer and a chaplain stood on her porch. She felt her body melt like Jell-O.

The wife of a career serviceman knew the protocol of informing military wives of their spouse's death. Screaming, she fell to her knees before they could utter a word.

"Are you Mrs. Sandra Jones, wife of Sergeant George Jones?" they asked, helping her to her feet.

Trembling, she whispered through the tears, "Yes, sir. I am."

"The Commandant of the United States Army has entrusted me to express his deep regret. Mrs. Jones, I am sorry to inform you that your husband, Sergeant George Jones lost his life in a roadside bombing at 1830 last night. He was a good soldier Ma'am."

Her sobbing drowned out the ability to hear the details of their announcement. Aware of this, they stayed with her, coaching her through the dreaded call to her mom and the plea for comfort. She was still in that doorway when Garrison found her.

"Hey, Mom, why didn't you come to wake me up and turn the alarm off?" Seeing the officers departing the house, he then really looked at his mom. As tears dripped off her chin, he knelt beside her and said, "Why are you crying? What is wrong? Why is Grandma coming up the driveway?"

Sandy's attention snapped back to the present when Officer Patterson addressed the group. "May I have your attention?" All eyes riveted on him when he lifted his cellphone. "Chief Daniels says they were delayed but are on the way."

In anticipation of the chief's arrival, the room fell into tense silence, with everyone staring at the door. When Daniels finally walked into the conference room, he could feel all their eyes upon him.

"Parents, I know you are anxious to hear details about the attack on your children. Unfortunately, I can't tell you everything, but I'll share what I can." He pulled a note from his pocket and put his glasses on to read it. "From what we understand, a student may have entered the school during 2nd period and made their way to Mr. Hughes' classroom. After an altercation, it appears several students were injured. That is all I can tell you right now. I will have more information to share at the next update."

Gathering her courage, Sandy stood up and asked, "Who did this, Chief? What is his name?"

"I am not at liberty to share that information at this time, ma'am," he told her. "Our deputies are taking statements and reviewing video footage as we speak."

By that time, Sandy was shaking with irrational anger. "Can't you tell us if our kids are alive? We deserve answers!"

Chief Daniels took a deep breath and slowly exhaled before responding to her. "Ma'am, I understand your need for information, but the doctors need time to triage the wounded to assess what is needed for each of the seven."

Sandy wasn't ready to give up. "So, you're saying seven people were injured? Tell us this then, is the unnamed attacker in custody?"

Again, Chief Daniels paused before answering, not wanting to compromise the investigation. "The attacker is in police custody and is no longer a threat. That is all I can tell you." He turned to leave but stopped when Sandy rose.

The group was talking amongst themselves when Sandy interrupted them loudly, spouting her thought. "I wonder what led up to this attack in the first place." Then she exclaimed, "I'll bet I know who did it!"

Meg put her arm on Sandy's shoulder and whispered, "Think about Garrison before you say something you will regret."

Vehemently she responded loud enough for the whole room to hear, "I AM THINKING OF MY SON! NO ONE SEEMS TO BE DOING ANYTHING, AND I NEED ANSWERS!" She said turning away from Meg fuming inside but not expressing it.

As if tag-teamed red-headed, Maureen held out her arms in a dramatic gesture and said, "Sandy's right, Chief, we want to know. Who did it?"

Before he could answer, Sandy took the floor, pacing back and forth in front of the other parents, sharing with them what she knew. "Last Friday, Garrison told me John Knowles argued with Mr. Hughes and then got suspended for it. Garrison felt sorry for him because John's dad, serving in Afghanistan, was injured, and is recovering at Walter

Reed Hospital. Anyway, Garrison tried to calm him down after school, but John just got angrier."

Yvonne Lynch, a tall blonde woman wearing too much makeup, said to the group, "John's mom Cynthia and I are friends. She told me that since her husband was injured, John has been a handful. So, I could reach out to her."

Thinking things were getting out of hand, Chief Daniels intervened. "Come now folks, I know you are frustrated, but let's stick to the facts we have at hand. Meanwhile, I'm going to check for an update."

When the Chief left, Chaplain Curtis asked if anyone wanted anything. Sandy snapped, "Yes, we want answers about our kids."

Seeing the other parents nod in agreement, Chaplain Curtis said, "Let's hope the Chief comes back with good news."

When Chief Daniels re-entered the conference room, he went straight to the chaplain. "Curtis, may I have a word with you, please out in the hall?"

Seeing the two men walk out together, Sandy signaled everyone to be quiet. Hoping to overhear their conversation, she cracked the door open no more than a fraction of an inch, then moved a chair next to it.

The Chief, who had long experience with distraught parents, moved his conversation with the chaplain to the end of the hallway. Safely out of hearing, he said, "Curtis, I spoke with Dr. Rodriguez just now. We lost two kids and the teacher, Mr. Hughes. He'll be out shortly to address the families, and it's our job to support him. Can you do that?"

"On my last tour of duty, which was in '07 in Iraq, we lost 904 American soldiers that year. I am used to praying over the bodies of fallen heroes, but to be honest, Chief I'm not experienced telling parents their kids were killed in a senseless attack."

Before the Chief could respond, Dr. Rodriquez came down the corridor to join them. Noting his solemn expression, the chaplain said, "You and I have announced the death of a loved one to family members many times, but never the death of innocent children to multiple parents. I don't know what to say."

"I understand. How about you offer a quick prayer to help us?"

"That, I can do." Chaplain Curtis prayed, "Dear God, please help us as we share this awful news with these families and give us the wisdom to be of help to them. Amen."

When they entered the conference room, all conversation in the group ceased as they turned to face the surgeon. Instinctively some held hands while others put their arms around one another to hear the news.

Knowing he was the bearer of bad news for some of them, the surgeon, spoke with compassion. "Parents, I am Dr. Rodriquez, the head surgeon here at Metro. I'm designated to tell you about your children. As I call the name of your child, please go to the adjoining room so we can speak privately," pointing to the frosted glass door to his left.

Unable to stay quiet any longer, Sandy spoke up. "When the military officer and chaplain showed up at my door to tell me that my husband died in action, I was alone. I don't know about the rest of you, but I don't want to be told bad news alone in a tiny cubicle. I want to be here, surrounded by all of you when he tells me about Garrison." The other parents nodded in agreement.

In response to their joint decision, the surgeon read the names on his clipboard, one at a time. "Let's begin with their teacher, Mr. Hughes. I spoke with his wife just now, and she gave me permission to tell you that he did not survive the attack."

Gasps and sobs rang out at the news. Finally, Sandy raised her voice to ask, "Can you tell us how he was killed, Dr. Rodriquez?"

When he answered, his voice was somber. "Mrs. Hughes said I could tell you he received a knife wound to the chest. That's all I can say." Giving them no time to process this loss, he moved on, "Is Mr. Dawson here?" When the slight, balding man acknowledged he was, he said, "Would you care to come into the consultation room for this, Mr. Dawson?"

"No, sir. I want you to tell me about my son out here with the others, please."

Pausing for a moment, the doctor said, "From the information our staff received while tending the students, your son Roger tried to stop the attacker. Unfortunately, his injuries were too severe, and he did not survive them. I'm sorry."

Mr. Dawson nodded on hearing the news about his son's death. Saying nothing at first, he closed his eyes tight, then stared straight ahead with tears streaming down his cheeks, and finally, as if reaching a crescendo, his body convulsed with gut-wrenching sobs and curse words spewed forth from his mouth as he slid to the floor.

Coach Adams came and sat on the floor beside him. Sandy put her arm on Sam Dawson's shoulder, rocking back and forth. Officer Patterson got up and knelt silently beside the grieving father, placing his palm on Mr. Dawson's knee until his own name was called.

"Officer Patterson, would you prefer to hear about your niece in the consultation room?"

Pulling away from Mr. Dawson, the officer drew in a deep breath before answering the surgeon. "No, thank you. I'd like to hear about my niece here with the others."

Dr. Rodriguez, with glistening eyes and a catch in his voice, told the officer, "Witnesses told our staff that Monique tried to help Mr. Hughes but got in the way of the assailant. I'm sorry, Mr. Patterson, but your niece's injuries were too severe; we couldn't save her."

Stunned by the news, Officer Patterson's gut-wrenching sobs moved everyone in the room. His niece Monique, who was like a daughter to him, was his responsibility while her mom was serving in Iraq. Now she was gone; how was he supposed to tell her mother? The remaining parents and guidance counselors sat frozen, unsure what to say or do.

Sensing the other parents' unspoken compassion for Mr. Dawson and Officer Patterson, but also their impatience to know about their own children, Sandy broke in, "Dr. Rodriquez, you've only named three victims. What about the other four?"

The surgeon looked down at his clipboard as though praying for wisdom, then turned back to her. "I have the rest of the list here, ma'am, but this is too important to rush. Now, the parents of Carmen Lynch?"

Yvonne raised a trembling hand, "Yes, I'm her mom. What can you tell me about my daughter?"

"Thankfully, Carmen's wounds were to her arms and legs. They were superficial, but she will require a course of antibiotics to prevent infection," said the doctor. "We'll keep her here overnight for observation and if she responds as expected, she can go home tomorrow."

Joyful her child's injuries weren't life-threatening, the relieved mom thanked the doctor, but he said, "I appreciate your kind words, but it wasn't just me in there—we had a complete team of medical professionals working to save those children and Mr. Hughes."

Clearing his throat, the doctor went on. "Are Tim Nelson's parents in the room?"

Coach Adams spoke up on Mrs. Nelson's behalf. "Tim's dad is deployed. I spoke with his mom, a teacher at the school. She took the day off because her youngest daughter is sick. She is waiting for her mother-in-law to arrive, so she asked me to keep her updated; please hold hers until she gets here."

Sandy interrupted, "Please tell me my son Garrison is next."

"Yes, Ma'am. He is."

Before he could go on, Chief Daniels interjected, "Dr. Rodriguez, may I speak before you proceed?"

"Yes, if it is alright with Ms. Jones," the doctor said.

With fear in her eyes, Sandy responded quickly, "If it's about my son, please just say it."

The Chief proceeded. "According to witness reports just received, Garrison tried to talk the attacker down, but without success. Instead of listening, the attacker shoved your son aside causing him to fall onto a glass shelf. The shelving broke on impact, and as a result, Garrison received severe cuts in the fall."

Frightened, Sandy stared at Dr. Rodriquez, afraid to hear his next words, "please, tell me, is my son alive?"

The surgeon nodded and said, "Your son lost a lot of blood when a shard of broken glass cut an artery. He is in surgery now, thanks in good part to one of his fellow students who knew how to apply pressure to stop the bleeding."

Dropping all pretense of bravery, Sandy sobbed onto her friend Meg's waiting shoulder. Beyond the surgeon's assurances, she had no way of knowing if Garrison would survive his injuries. She had already lost her husband; she did not know if she could survive losing her son, too.

Maureen Spencer looked around the room as if to gather courage before speaking. "What about my daughter, Amber Spencer? You have not called her name. What is her condition?"

The doctor nodded. "Yes, Ms. Spencer. Do you want to talk privately?"

"No, thank you. Like the others, I prefer to stay in here."

"Ma'am, your daughter was stabbed in the abdomen. She is still in surgery for maybe another three hours. I'd like to suggest you allow Chaplain Curtis to escort you to the family waiting room when you are ready."

In shock because of what she'd just heard, Maureen couldn't speak. Her daughter, the cheerleading squad captain, was fighting for her life while she and the others were sitting in the conference room waiting and drinking coffee. She felt helpless.

His list finished, the doctor turned to head back to the operating room, but the group still needed an answer to the one question nobody wanted to ask. Mr. Dawson rose, and in a voice choked with tears, said, "Before you leave, we'd like to know the identity and condition of the attacker. Who is he, and where is he being held?"

Dr. Rodriquez let out a prolonged sigh and turned to the Chief of Police. "Chief, can you answer Mr. Dawson's question?"

"Mr. Dawson, I am so sorry for your loss, and I know you and the others have questions. We will do our best to answer your questions when School Resource Officer

(SRO) Wilson gets here, which should be any minute now," Daniels told him. Then he turned to the others, saying, "This is a good time to take a break if you need to, but don't go far."

Learning Details

WILSON CAUTIOUSLY OPENED the conference room door. He felt responsible for not saving lives that morning and feared they would verbally and maybe even physically pounce on him when he entered the room. Instead, they stared at him in silence until Garrrison's mom spoke up.

"Officer Wilson, thank you for what you tried to do to help our kids today, but we deserve to know about their attacker. Who is he?"

Relieved they were not going to attack him; the school officer looked to Chief Daniels for guidance. When his superior officer nodded, he told them, "He is one of their classmates, and his name is John Knowles."

Some parents gasped, and others cursed when they heard John's name, but Sandy declared, "I knew it was him! I told you earlier that John is the friend of Garrison's whose dad is at Walter Reed.

Receiving the green light to proceed, Officer Wilson continued, "John is being guarded in a secure location here in the hospital."

Sandy asked, "Has John's mom been notified?" She must be shocked.

Officer Wilson looked to his Chief again before answering, knowing the information was already leaked by witnesses in multiple text and tweet messages. "Yes, all notifications were handled before we released the information to you.

Dr. Rodriquez apologetically responded to Mr. Dawson. "Parents, we live in an Army base town. Our loved ones go into harm's way every day. We know when we kiss them good-bye that we may not see them alive again, but we do not expect that with our children. Today we suffered a great loss. It is not just your child, Mr. Dawson, or your niece Officer Patterson, or Mr. Hughes. It is the loss of innocence and the sense of security for all our children."

Chaplain Curtis added, "I don't believe under normal circumstances John would have done this horrific act. But, before you judge his actions, think about his stress, and his fears that his wounded dad would never recover."

Mr. Dawson, retired Army Sergeant, stared unblinking at the chaplain and said, "That's a great speech, but that does not bring back my son, Roger. I taught him to respect others and to listen. He did what I told him to do, and now he is dead."

Dr. Rodriquez turned back to face the room and Mr. Dawson. "You are right, Mr. Dawson. I am sorry. Let me go back and do what I know how to do best, using these," holding up his hands, "to help heal bodies and to supervise my colleagues doing the same. Again, I am sorry for your losses, and I will be praying for all of you."

As Sandy and Meg tried to comfort Officer Patterson, Mr. Dawson stood up and cleared his throat. "I don't know about the rest of you, but I believe this could have been prevented, and I am going to find out what went wrong if it takes me the rest of my life," he said, pounding his fist into his palm.

Numbed Resource Officer Wilson looked Mr. Dawson in the eye and said, "If you're blaming me, you don't have to. I already do."

Principal Edwards sat motionless, fearing he would be blamed and fired over the situation. Chaplain Curtis intervened. "Parents, emotions are running high. Let us wait until we see what comes out about all this."

Before finishing his sentence, Anita, Tim's mom, entered the conference room like a mother on a mission to confront the bully who hurt her son. "Where is he?" she screamed. "I have to see my baby boy!"

Chaplain Curtis diverted his attention to extinguish this new brush fire. He extended his hand to greet Anita. She pulled back and barked, "And who are you? And unless you can tell me about my son, Tim, I have nothing to say to you."

After inhaling deeply, Chaplain Curtis retracted his hand and responded, "I'm Chaplain Curtis. Dr. Rodriquez was here about 10 minutes ago and returned to surgery."

"Okay, Chaplain Curtis, you trot your butt out of here and go find out about my son," she said while shooing him out the door with her hand.

Chaplain Curtis went to the front desk and asked Janice to page Dr. Rodriquez to tell him a parent had arrived and to please come talk to her as soon as he could. Chaplain Curtis did not immediately return to the conference room, but instead went to the men's room to relieve himself and splash cold water on his face. When Curtis signed up for the military, he envisioned counseling soldiers amid battle, not comforting grieving parents who just lost their child due to a disgruntled student. Now, as a retired Army chaplain, he was experiencing the most difficult mission in his career. Gathering courage after a short prayer, he headed back to the battleground.

He approached Tim's mom, who was pacing and loudly crackling her wad of gum. "Mother of Tim."

"My name is Anita if you must know. So, what'd you find out?"

"Ma'am, Dr. Rodriquez is in surgery. Receptionist Janice paged him. He will come out when he can."

"Not good enough. Go back and page the hospital administrator. If you can't do that, I will go find the person myself."

"Yes, Ma'am. I will do what I can." Relieved to be out of her way, he slowly went to the chaplaincy office and called his supervisor. He relayed the events and current situation. Chaplain Mike agreed to come down and see if he could help calm the waters.

Chaplin Curtis prayed. *God, Ms. Anita reminds me of my dad, Colonel Russell. If he were only alive to see me now, wouldn't he be surprised? I wonder how his stoic nature would handle this situation. I wish I could call my boyfriend for support, but someone might hear me, and no one at work knows I am gay. Would you please guide me? Thanks, Amen.*

In the meantime, Dr. Rodriquez took a break from surgery to return to the conference room, where parents were milling around texting and calling family and friends. He visually surveyed the sea of faces in the room, looking for anyone he had not yet spoken to. Anita strode up to him and said, "You must be the doc, saving our kids. I hope you're not saving that SOB who hurt my child."

Ignoring her comment, the doctor said, "Hello, I am Dr. Rodriquez. Are you the parent of an injured child? If so, we can go in the consultation room to talk privately."

"I'm Tim's mom, Anita. I don't need a consultation room. Just tell me, am I planning a funeral or college for my Tim?"

"Ms. Anita, your son Tim has a stab wound to the chest, but it is not life-threatening. He is conscious now after surgery, and you can see him in about two hours."

Relieved, Anita collapsed into the closest chair and buried her head in her hands, letting the façade of being an aggressive confronter fade.

As the occupants of the conference room let the shock settle in, Sandy went into action. Leaning over to her friend, she said loud enough for others to hear, "Meg, could you go to the cafeteria and bring back some sandwiches for everyone? Here is my charge card. We need to eat to keep our strength up."

Refusing to accept the card, Meg glared at her as she whispered in her ear, "Sandy, you can't afford to do that! If people are hungry, they can tend to themselves. I'm scared you're spiraling into a manic phase again. Please think about what you are doing. Garrison needs his mom to be stable."

"Meg, I know you think I have gone off the rails, but I am just trying to keep busy, so I don't go mad with worry."

"Okay, Meg said, slowing down her voice, "but please check with me before you make such a costly offer again. I'm telling you as your concerned friend. You can't afford to pay for everyone's meal. You just told me this morning you only have $50 in your checking account to last until payday."

"Fine, Meg, but you're not my parent."

"That's right, Sandy, but I am thinking of your last manic debacle and how it affected everyone who cares about you. Think of Garrison and how you will need to have money to pay hospital bills and medicines and stuff."

Curtis spoke up, resolving this issue. "Parents, the mobile food cart will be here shortly. You are welcome to select what you wish compliments of the hospital." Sandy put her card back in her wallet.

Maureen and Anita said they weren't hungry and left together to wait in the surgery waiting room. As the two worried moms huddled in the corner of the waiting area,

Anita began to hyperventilate. Maureen tried to comfort her by handing her a tissue, getting her a cup of water, and offering to call someone.

One of the pink ladies handing out magazines saw Anita gasping for air and asked if she could help. Suffering herself from anxiety, she knew a panic attack when she saw one. She invited Anita to go into the adjoining cubicle. As the volunteer rubbed her back, Anita calmed down.

Anita said, "I'm sorry. This whole situation reminds me of the trauma I went through when I was 16."

The pink lady said nothing, just listened with her eyes. Anita presented the details.

"Whenever my dad was home from deployment, he stayed drunk. He would take out his anger on my mom because she couldn't read his mind fast enough to know what he wanted before he did. One morning when my mom came home from her second job, dad was sitting at the kitchen table drunk. He began cursing under his breath, saying she was sleeping around on him. She yelled and said if he provided for the family instead of boozing all the time, she would be home. He got angrier. I was trying to get out before the violence began.

"My school bus was waiting outside. The driver honked to tell me he was there. I opened the door and signaled for him to wait a minute. I was worried about my nine-month-old brother Tommy asleep in his crib. I was the first stop on the route, so I knew I had to hurry. I was afraid to go knowing my dad would beat her into unconsciousness again and no one would be there for

Tommy. I put my hand on the screen's doorknob to leave but heard Mom rummaging in the hall closet for something. I froze. She returned with a baseball bat. I yelled, 'Mom, don't do it!' Mom started swinging the bat in the air around the table. Dad tried to grab it but was too drunk and fell to the floor, hitting his head. I screamed, and Mom went numb. The bus driver heard me. He dashed into the house breathlessly asking, 'Is everything alright?'

"Seeing Dad on the floor not moving, I took over. I told the bus driver, 'I need to call 911. We don't have a phone. I'm going to my neighbor's. You stay with my mom.'

"They arrested Mom for dad's death. I testified at the hearing telling all the incidents that Dad beat my mom so badly her face was unrecognizable. The prosecutor convinced the jury that my mom planned to kill this decorated Army vet. She served ten years in prison.

"A local Baptist church family took my brother and me in, providing us comfort and security we never had. I learned to speak up and not become a victim like my mom. She never recovered emotionally and chose a series of men like my father when she got out. Now my son Tim is the victim of a crime, and I was not there to protect him. Whenever there is a crisis, I go into overdrive to hide my fear, she said, sobbing."

The pink lady just held her and let her cry it out until eventually, Anita was able to return to her seat next to Yvonne.

Upon re-entering the conference room, Captain Daniels released Officer Patterson to go home and make final arrangements for his niece Monique. Mr. Dawson sat in the corner, dazed. He did not have anywhere to go and no one to contact. Divorced for a decade, he raised Roger by himself after his son's mom ran off with a Navy pilot, never to be heard from again.

Sandy knew Sam well: he lived two doors down from her, and their sons played on the same baseball team. She walked over to him and spoke softly. "Sam, I am so sorry about Roger."

Sam snapped back to reality. "Huh, what'd you say?"

Putting her hand on his arm, she repeated what she had said. He looked at her with tear-stained cheeks. "What am I going to do without him?"

Sandy said, "Remember when my George died two years ago, you talked to me and told me I was not alone? You said you would be there for me until I no longer needed you. Sometimes I would call you at four in the morning because I couldn't sleep, and you would always answer."

Sam said, "Of course, you needed me, and a promise is a promise."

"Well, Sam. We will get through this together. I will be there for you just like you were there for me. I promise. Besides, I don't know what the outcome of Garrison's condition will be, so I need you too. We are in this together."

Sam thanked her and said he was going to go home and just sit in Roger's room for a while. Sandy agreed to check on him later. Just then, a nurse came into the conference room and asked for Sandy.

The nurse escorted Sandy to the same waiting room where Maureen and a now calm Anita were sitting. As she approached them, the two women looked up apprehensively. Sandy wondered if either of them had received any update about their child's condition. It was as if they were forming a silent bond in being part of a club no one wanted to join.

The nurse asked Sandy to wait in the small cubicle beside the communal coffee pot. *Why is there always coffee involved in every stressful situation in my life? Is it to torture me, to remind me that I never want a cup again?*

Just then, Dr. Rodriquez entered the room smiling. *That must be a good sign.*

"Ms. Jones. Garrison is out of surgery. I have repaired the artery with a graft, and we are giving him a transfusion. He is heavily sedated. He will need to be on antibiotics to prevent any infection. Your son is a lucky young man. An inch further in either direction and he would not have survived his injury. You can see your son in about two hours. We should have him stabilized by then."

Sandy wept openly after she heard those words, but when the surgeon asked if she had any questions, she blew her nose then replied with a sniff. "Yes, I have a couple.

First, my son is friends with John Knowles and my guess is that his mom is probably not here yet. Am I right? If that's the case, is it appropriate for me to speak with John?"

"Ma'am, that is something I have no control over. You'll need to ask Chief Daniels."

Sandy thanked him. "I'm going to go back to the conference room to see if the Chief is still there. Can you text me or have someone come get me when I can see Garrison?"

"Yes, of course! If you give me your number, I will have his nurse give you a call when he can be seen." With her number safely in his contacts list, he patted his pocket and went back to check on his patients.

Mission Engaged

WITH THE MANY spinning parts in place, Sandy felt the need to shift her attention to John Knowles. She knew what it was like to be blindsided with bad news. Cynthia had more than a full plate. Even though a part of her was angry that John tried to kill Garrison, she knew this was not the John she had known for the last five years. Her years of working at Oasis Mental Health Center and going through grief counseling there taught her to see people for who they were, not for what is wrong with them.

Chief Daniels was about to leave the conference room as Sandy entered. "Chief, may I speak with you in the hall, please?"

"Yes, Ma'am. I was just on my way back to the station."

Nervous about what she was to impart, Sandy's heart sped up as she whispered to the Chief, "I have confidential information about John Knowles that I could not share in the conference room with the other parents."

"What's that?" the Chief said, leaning in to hear.

"I work for the Oasis Mental Health Center in the budgeting and insurance billing department. This morning I came across an invoice for an MRI the staff psychiatrist ordered for John with the attached report. Unfortunately, Chief Daniels, John is not well—he has a brain tumor. His mom has not been told yet because she is tending to her husband recovering in Walter Reed from his Afghanistan war-related injuries. John was already scheduled to come in this Friday afternoon for the results. I doubt that Dr. Jacobs, the psychiatrist, knows about this incident or has seen the report yet. Normally, I could not share this information because of HIPAA (Health Insurance Portability Accountability Act) rules, but the continuing education class I took for my job spells out this exception."

Chief Daniels scratched his head and sighed. "This could change everything. Can you contact Dr. Jacobs and have him call me?"

"Sure, let me see what I can do." Sandy went back inside the conference room and pulled Meg outside to discuss the situation privately. Meg agreed to inform Dr. Jacobs and get him to contact the Chief.

When Meg left to talk to Dr. Jacobs, Sandy pondered her next step. Though her own son was not yet out of the woods, John Knowles had no one there for him at that moment. She knew if he were thinking clearly, he would not have committed such a heinous act, so she decided to do some snooping on her own. With her mind racing, she began by wandering the hospital floor by floor looking for a law enforcement officer guarding a room.

On the sixth floor, when she meandered down the north, south, west, and finally the east corridor, she found what she was looking for: in front of the last room on the right, a guard sat beside the door. At that point, it occurred to her that more than one person might be held in a room. *What if I get inside and it's not John, but another aggressive and dangerously crazed person?*

Approaching the guard with small talk she said, "Officer Thompson (reading his badge). I'm Sandy Jones. Chief Daniels sent me to talk to John Knowles."

"Mrs. Jones," he told her respectfully, "I have gotten no communication about you seeing Mr. Knowles from the Chief."

Sandy smiled warmly and replied, "Well, you can call him if you like. I'll wait right here." *Glad I got the right room.*

Feeling proud of herself for figuring out where John was being held, she waited for the officer to make the call. But unfortunately, he spoke so softly into the phone, she couldn't hear the conversation. Then he turned to her, saying, "Ma'am, the Chief wants to talk to you."

Gingerly taking the phone, she answered, "This is Sandy Jones, Chief."

Chief responded in a gruff tone of voice, "I know you think you're helping Mrs. Jones, but what you are doing could jeopardize this whole investigation. The suspect is not to receive visitors."

Quickly resetting her course, she said, "Chief, John knows and trusts me and, since I have known this kid five years, I know this is not who he is. I'm sure he is scared, especially since his mom isn't here yet. If you allow me to see him, I will only go in for one minute, and Officer Thompson can record what I say. I only need to deliver a message to him; I will not interfere with the investigation."

"And what might this message be, Ms. Jones?"

"I want to tell John that his mom is on the way, and that his psychiatrist, Dr. Jacobs, will talk to him soon. I need to clear it with her first, but I believe she will agree with me. John needs to be told there is a medical reason he did this attack, and he must follow whatever Dr. Jacobs tells him to do."

"Ms. Jones, I do not believe Mr. Knowles is receptive to input from anyone right now. I've already told you I will consider his psychiatrist talking to him if he contacts me first. Let Dr. Jacobs handle talking to John's mom. That is not your responsibility."

"Okay, fine. My co-worker Meg is having Dr. Jacobs paged. He is either making rounds here in the Psych ward or back at Oasis. She is retrieving the report from my desk, and I'll text Cynthia to expect a call from Dr. Jacobs." She said, ignoring the Chief's order for her to stop taking matters into her own hands.

"Well, as soon as I hear from Dr. Jacobs, I will make a decision about what to do and not before. Do you understand?"

"Yes, of course, but I forgot to ask you for the best number for Dr. Jacobs to reach you," she said pulling a pen and scrap piece of paper out of her pocket.

"My work number is 540-555-4242," he told her. "Tell him to call and leave a message if I don't answer."

Just as she finished texting Cynthia to explain the latest developments, she got a call from within the hospital. "Hello, this is Sandy Jones," she answered.

"Ms. Jones, I'm Mary, a nurse from the surgical floor," the nurse told her. "You can see your son now. If you go to the nurse's station on the 5th floor South, they will direct you to his room."

When Sandy got off the elevator the CNA at the front desk directed her to the last room on the left. Not knowing what she'd find, she carefully opened the door and peeked in. Her son Garrison was hooked up to IV antibiotics dripping into his left arm, blood transfusing into the right arm. She tiptoed over to the bed and kissed him on the top of his head, something she'd done ever since he was a baby.

He opened one bruised eye and said, "Hi, Mom, I'm glad you're here. I'm so sorry."

Surprised at his words, she asked, "What are you sorry for, Son?"

"First Dad died, and now here I am sliced up and plugged into IVs. And you are probably pissed at me for getting involved in that fight. But Mom, you gotta understand, I really tried to stop John, but he was out of control. I have never seen him like that."

"Garrison, it's okay," she said, stroking his forehead."
I don't blame you for anything, but I am glad you tried
to help your friend. I spoke with your doctor—he said
everything will be alright with you, but it will take time
to heal. As for John, let's save that talk for later. What you
need right now is rest."

Fighting to keep his eyes open, Garrison turned
to Sandy, his words already heavy with sleep. "I love
you, Mom."

"I love you too, sweetheart," she told him. "Rest now."
She sat in the chair beside his bed, her knees knocking
from anxiety-induced mania as he began to snore. She
stroked his arm, praying and thanking God her son was
alive and would recover, hoping this prayer of gratitude
would calm her as well.

Unfortunately, the meds she'd taken earlier were beginning to wear off, and with the adrenaline still pumping
through her body she became even more restless. I simply
cannot be still, she thought to herself. *God, please take care
of Garrison and forgive me for leaving him to check on John.
I remember what it is like to be in a crisis and all alone.
Someone must help him, and why not me, who has been
through it?*

Certain Garrison was resting comfortably, Sandy
crept out of his room, checking to see if anyone might be
watching, then bounded up the steps. Reaching the 6th
floor, she pulled the heavy door open, then peeped out to
see if the guard was still sitting watch. He was, with Dr.
Jacobs standing nearby speaking earnestly into his phone.

She assumed he was speaking to Chief Daniels. Thinking of a good reason to present herself, she strode confidently toward them.

Waiting until he ended the call, she said, "Hello, Dr. Jacobs. I'm Sandy Jones from the billing department at Oasis. May I speak with you privately for a minute?"

Frowning, he said, "Certainly, Mrs. Jones. I recognize you. It appears the stress of today's events has blurred your judgment. You are bordering on violating the HIPAA regulations."

Unphased by his disapproval, she spoke quickly. "I know I should have approached you first, but you are right—I was too stressed to think of the proper procedure. I'm terribly sorry."

Noting Sandy's agitated expression, the psychiatrist's first task was to calm her down. "Ms. Jones, under the circumstances, it's acceptable that you revealed John's medical information, but I must take it from here, or there could be fines levied on you and Oasis. My priority right now is to reach John's mother; I need her permission to see him before I can proceed."

When Dr. Jacobs began searching his notes for Cynthia's number, Sandy told him, "Our families have been friends and neighbors for years, so I've already called her. Here is her number-she's expecting your call. By the way, are you aware John's father was injured in Afghanistan? He's at Walter Reed right now. That's where Cynthia was when the school attack occurred." Shaking his head in wonder, he walked over to a more private corner to dial Cynthia's number.

Her mission accomplished; Sandy was unsure what to do next, so she waited nearby. Curious about what Dr. Jacobs was saying to John's mom she listened closely, but his words were muffled. She was surprised when the doctor beckoned her to his side. Unsure what he wanted, she half-expected to be either chastised or praised, but she obeyed the summons.

More than anything, Sandy wanted to reassure John's mom that she would do what she could to help John until she could reach the hospital. As it turned out, John's mom, Cynthia, wanted to speak with her, too.

Cynthia seemed quite level-headed on the phone, considering the circumstances. "Sandy, thank you for sharing John's information with Dr. Jacobs. I sensed something was not right with him, but I have been preoccupied with his dad at Walter Reed. John trusts you, as do I. If you are willing, I will grant permission for you to be in the room when Dr. Jacobs speaks to John, but only if I can participate via speakerphone. Are you okay with that?"

With permission granted, the guard, Dr. Jacobs, and Sandy entered John's room. They found him awake and handcuffed to the bedrail with his hair covered in caked blood. He looked frightened at their entry, but he recognized Sandy immediately.

Officer Thompson pushed the record button on his phone, then explained to the accused boy what he was going to do. "Mr. Knowles, I'm Officer Thompson. Your mother has given Mrs. Jones permission to be present in her absence as your doctor talks to you. Your mom is on speaker with Dr. Jacobs. Therefore, I must ask your permission to record our conversations. Are you okay with that?"

Looking perplexed, John responded with a murmured "Okay," then turned to Sandy for answers to his own questions. "Ms. Jones, what has happened? And why am I handcuffed to the bed? Why are there bandages on my wrists . . . and these?" he asked, pulling at the cuffs.

Dr. Jacobs spoke, "Hello, John, remember me? I am Dr. Jacobs, your psychiatrist."

Looking confused, John just blankly stared as Dr. Jacobs continued. "I sent you for an MRI because of your headaches, angry outbursts, and sleep issues. Do you recall that?"

John furrowed his brow as if trying to retrieve what the doctor was saying but did not respond.

"Okay, I need you to answer a more important question. Do you remember what happened this morning?"

Glancing first at Sandy for encouragement, the frightened boy said, "No, sir. All I can remember is the horrible headache I had when I got up this morning. I remember going to the school and being mad, but the rest is a blur."

Her face and voice gentle now, Sandy leaned over the bedrail to put her hand on his arm. "John, it is true, you had an MRI with Dr. Jacobs, and he found something on your brain. He wants to tell both you and your mom about it right now. Remember she's on speakerphone with us. Would you like to say something to her?"

Staring into the phone in Dr. Jacobs' hand, John said, "Hi, Mom."

"Hello, John. I love you, son. I promise we'll get through this together, okay?"

Mumbling, John said, "Okay, sure." But then he turned back to the doctor with a confused expression. "Why are you here?"

"Thanks to the MRI, we know the reason you've been having headaches, forgetting things, and losing your temper. You have a tumor in the left temporo-parietal lobe of your brain; that's what is causing your symptoms. We will treat it with surgery and radiation soon, but first, we must tend to the reason for those handcuffs."

His eyes big, John stammered, "Wh . . .what did I do?"

Sandy, looking first to Dr. Jacobs for permission but not waiting to receive it, said gently, "John, you hurt some people."

John teared up when he heard the news. "Oh, my God, what did I do? Are they alright?"

Knowing John's response was sincere, Dr. Jacobs patted his patient on the top of the head, "I think you've heard enough, for now, so we'll tell you more about it later. Let's get your treatment started first."

He turned to leave the room, phone in hand, when Cynthia's voice came through. "May I speak for a moment, Dr. Jacobs?"

Startled when he realized John's mother was still on the other end, the doctor turned to John and Sandy to get their attention. "I'm sorry, Mrs. Knowles, I wasn't ignoring you. Please speak."

"John, honey, remember, I love you, and I am on my way there as fast as I can. I am sorry I have not been there for you because I have been helping Dad recover. We will get through this together, okay?"

John answered, "Mom, I'm scared. Please come soon."

Cynthia responded, "Sure, son, as fast as I can go without getting a speeding ticket, okay?" she said, choking back tears. Then she turned her attention to Dr. Jacobs. "Thank you for helping my son. Please tell me what is next."

Dr. Jacobs explained what was required and that it needed to be instituted quickly before the tumor grew any larger. Sandy gently squeezed John's hand as Dr. Jacobs reassured him that he would begin work immediately on getting the necessary approvals to start treatment.

Before they hung up, Sandy reassured Cynthia that she would try to stop by John's room as much as possible until she arrived. When Dr. Jacobs left, the guard turned off the recording, saving it for Chief Daniels' review.

John was sobbing when they left his room. He pleaded with Sandy, trying to get her to stay behind, but she couldn't—she knew Garrison needed her, too. Her motherly heart ached for John, all the victims, and for the already distraught Cynthia heading back from tending her sick husband at Walter Reed to handle the situation with her son.

Outside John's room, Dr. Jacobs thanked Sandy for her bravery and for getting involved when Chief Daniels appeared in the hallway. Feeling a part of the team by then, Sandy leaned against the wall and waited when Officer Thompson handed the Chief his cellphone with an earbud.

After listening to the recorded conversation, Chief Daniels asked if the boy had an attorney, explaining the necessity of a lawyer to request the psychiatric evaluation Dr. Jacobs suggested. Then, to her surprise, he turned to Sandy.

"Mrs. Jones, while I don't care for the way you inserted yourself into John's case, I realize now it was for the best. You are free to return to your son."

"Thanks, Chief." Then she surprised them all. "Sir, if it is all the same to you, I'll come back periodically to check on John until his mom arrives. I promised her that I would, and with your permission, I mean to keep that promise. I know I can't speak to him privately, but I want him to know that he will have support. He is only fourteen years old and scared. I remember how frightened I was when I heard about my husband's death. That's when I promised God if I ever could help someone else the way I was helped, I would. I think this is it."

The Chief rubbed his temples, trying to ease the tension from all the decisions he had to make that day without much forethought. He turned to Sandy, "Ms. Jones, I normally would not allow someone to be involved but this case is anything but normal. Dr. Jacobs agrees John needs to know he's not alone, so if you're dropping by helps keep John calm and cooperative, you may enter when a nurse is taking his vitals. The officer on duty must accompany you and record any conversations you may have. You are not to bring up any details of the case. Is that understood?"

Speaking calmly (a second Lamictal thirty minutes before lessened her frenetic behavior), Sandy said, "Yes, sir. I will follow your instructions to the letter. Thank you."

Since she now understood the necessity of an attorney for John, Sandy called his mom back, "Cynthia, Chief Daniels just asked if you have an attorney. If not, I have an attorney friend—Megan Powell. Would you like me to call her on your behalf? She's the lawyer who helped me acquire my benefits after my husband's service-connected death."

Cynthia had not thought about the legal ramifications of John's act of violence and agreed to have Sandy contact the attorney. Then, after checking on Garrison, she informed Dr. Jacobs of the update. "Megan Powell's credentials are impeccable, Dr. Jacobs. She graduated in the top ten percent of her class at George Mason University and served on the United States Court of Appeals for the Armed Forces until her retirement. In addition, her father was a Virginia Supreme Court Justice. Also, because she receives military retirement benefits, she serves pro bono clientele on occasion." Pausing to let the information sink in, Sandy added. "And as if that were not enough, Megan commands respect in this military town for representing wounded warriors seeking their rightful benefits."

"So, this legal paragon lives here, in our town?" Dr. Jacobs asked.

"Yes, she does, and I'm going to call her tonight!" Sandy told him. "I will let you know what she says first thing in the morning."

That night, when Sandy called her friend, she agreed to take the case pro bono if John's mom agreed. Sandy called Cynthia who was just about back in town. "Hey, Cynthia how are you holding up?"

"I'm numb. Going on autopilot," Cynthia replied. "I've got about twenty miles to go. So, tell me, what did you hear from the attorney?"

Sandy updated Cynthia on the conversation with attorney Powell and her agreement to serve pro bono. She then told her she would be checking on John per the instructions Chief Daniels provided.

"I cannot thank you enough for your help, Sandy," Cynthia told her. "As awful as this situation with John's violence is, we'd be lost without your help. Can you text attorney Powell's number to me? I know I will need to sign paperwork to get this process started."

Cynthia called the police station as she entered town to ask the procedure to visit John. The Chief spoke with her personally and agreed to meet her at the hospital. Silence reigned as they rode the elevator together to the sixth floor. Cynthia was devoid of words. The Chief had a mixture of emotions, anger, sadness, bewilderment, and fear all swirling in his head. If he did not handle this case right, he could be out of a job next election. Daniels stood in the doorway as Cynthia tried to comfort her son in his confusion. Exhausted, she promised to come back as soon as allowed knowing each visit had a 10-minute limit.

Getting only three hours of restless sleep Cynthia met with attorney Powell at 8 am the next morning to sign the legal forms to represent John, and a release to gain access to John's medical records at Oasis.

With the signed paperwork in hand, the attorney contacted Chief Daniels to let him know she would represent John Knowles. Then she reached out to her former classmate Judge Murphy to get an order to schedule the forensic assessment. He granted permission for her to be in the room when it was conducted but not to interfere. She agreed.

The Next Seventy-Two Hours

THE MORNING AFTER the Greenwood Middle School attack, Sandy read the Twitter post announcing a memorial service in the school gym at 7 pm that evening for Roger, Monique, and Mr. Hughes. In addition, local radio and television stations broadcast the story, spreading it even further. She turned off her radio to avoid the overstimulation. She was pleased to hear that Mr. Adams, the Varsity basketball coach, and a part-time preacher, would conduct the service, since he was instrumental in helping Garrison recover from his dad's death.

Later that morning, Dr. Robinson, Sandy's personal therapist, sent her a text. "I think we need to have a session before the memorial service. Please call me."

When they met at 3 pm, his eyes widened when he noticed her disheveled state.

Her hands fidgeting, she opened with the obvious, "Dr. Robinson, I know you see me in this manic state, but under the circumstances, don't you think anyone would?"

"Sandy, this isn't about just anyone; it's about you and being stable enough to handle Garrison's situation. He needs you now more than ever. So, let's revisit what happened to you, and separate that from what is happening now, okay?"

Eyes downcast, she surrendered. "Yeah, I guess so."

"Tell me again the details about your dad when you were 16 and we will parse it out together."

Inhaling deeply, Sandy retrieved the horrible memory of that day, reciting the details of that night in a monotone. "I went out that night and was supposed to be home at 11 pm from my date. I was ten minutes late because we took the long way back to avoid the heavy fog by the lake, that's when we were stopped by a long freight train. When I opened the front door and turned on the light, the first thing I saw was my dad sitting in the recliner. I wondered how long he'd been waiting for me in the dark. He lifted his hand out of his robe pocket, pointed his pistol at me, and said, "Whore, that's what you are. You're a Whore!"

When my mom heard the commotion, she shuffled from the bedroom in her slippers and robe. Dad turned the gun on her and said, "You're both in cahoots with the devil. You think I'm crazy but I'm not. I'm going to end this right now." Mom and I watched as he turned the gun around and as if in slow motion, opened his mouth and pulled the trigger.

When she finished the retelling, Sandy stared off into space with her eyes glazed over frozen in the flashback of seeing her dad complete his suicide.

"Okay, come back to the room. Tell me three things you see." She returned to the present following his instructions. "Now tell me about your first psychotic episode."

"The first time it happened was just after my dad was diagnosed with schizoaffective disorder. Mom tells me, when it happened, I went to school talking gibberish one day and started eating flowers from the school's garden. I had just turned 14. My homeroom teacher called in the school nurse, and the paramedics delivered me to the psych ward. I don't remember anything until later when I was on meds. I missed that whole school year."

"Fine recall, Sandy," the doctor told her. "Now tell me three things you can touch."

Emerging from the fog she said, "My feet on the floor, my arm on my knee, and my butt in the chair."

"Good, let's compare then and now: how old is Garrison?"

"He's 14, and so is John, the boy who stabbed them."

"Yes, but just because they are the age you were when this happened to you, doesn't mean it is the same situation as yours was."

"I know, but like my mom who was too fragile to help me after dad committed suicide, so is Cynthia, John's mom, with her husband being in Walter Reed and all."

"Yes, though that may be true, why do you feel it is your job to step in and take over everything? Dr. Jacobs filled me in on how you were trying to get in to see John to 'help'."

"It's because I know how he feels! That kid is scared; he's like me when I was hospitalized, and like when my dad killed himself. Somebody must help him, so why not me who's been there?"

"But Sandy, you are not a trained professional. You do not know how to distinguish what is helping him from what is complicating the situation. Your wounds are not healed yet. So, let's come up with a plan, okay?"

"What kind of plan?" Sandy asked.

"This is a plan for now, I am going to up your Lamictal to two (200 mg), one in the morning and one at night. Anything more you want to do, run it by me first, okay? If you need to take some time off from work, you have your Family Medical Leave Act in place. Can your mom come stay with you for a while and help? Didn't you tell me she recovered from your dad's suicide with trauma therapy? I'm sure she'd understand. How about your friend Sam? Can you talk to him?"

Nodding her head in agreement, Sandy said, "Sam can't help me right now, because his son Roger was one of the casualties. He needs me, so I want to be there for him."

Before Dr. Robinson called Sandy's prescription into the local pharmacy, he asked how her son Garrison was doing.

"He's stable right now, but he's got a long road ahead of him."

In the afternoon staff meeting, he shared the plan of how they could all help keep Sandy mentally stable. Everyone agreed she was a valuable employee, and they would work with her as best they could if she followed Dr. Robinson's instructions.

Sorrow cast a dark shadow over the grieving friends and family members gathered at the memorial service. As the service commenced under the direction of Coach Adams, everyone in the large gymnasium teared up during his talk. Emotions ran high when the school chorus sang "Amazing Grace," the uniformed cheerleading squad sobbed loudly for their lost classmates and recovering fellow cheerleader Amber Spencer; they had no way of knowing if she would fully recover from her stab wound to cheer with them again. On the overhead screen, pictures scrolled of the deceased students and their teacher, Mr. Hughes. Seeing the video brought back vivid memories of the teacher and the classmates they'd lost, evoking both loud wails from the crowd, sometimes followed by subdued chuckles at some of the antics they saw played out on the screen. When Principal Edwards addressed the crowd, however, there was total silence. "Students, parents, and loved ones, we are here to honor your lost classmates and beloved teacher. There are no words to say that will ease our sorrow right now, but I believe that if they could, Roger, Monique, and Mr. Hughes would tell us to march on and learn from this tragedy. I know I will," he said, tearing up before sitting down.

At the conclusion of the service, Coach Adams offered a closing prayer. After, he made an announcement: "Students, family members, and faculty, thank you for coming. Now Chief Daniels will answer safety and security questions for any of you who choose to stay." No one left.

Though those involved in the case were sworn to silence, a few days later, a hospital employee leaked details about John's medical condition to the press. She was promptly fired, but it was too late: once posted on her Facebook page social media picked up the story. From there, stories spread like wildfire, including a rumor the attack was a hoax. Those who believed John was responsible for his behavior, medical condition or not, were angry. They hounded Chief Daniel's office for answers to questions like where the boy was being held, and when the trial would begin, but that information was safely withheld.

Without violating the HIPAA regulations, she was reminded of in a recent staff meeting, Sandy did what she could to dispel the outright lies she heard. At the meeting it was made clear that if she shared information about John's medical condition gleaned from his electronic record, she could be fired and personally sued, and her own life and that of Garrison's ruined. The mental health center would be forced to pay a fine for the damages her leak of information might cause, and the executives could possibly go to jail. She couldn't let that happen.

Sandy's mother voiced her opinion, too. "I can't understand why you don't want this criminal prosecuted as an adult; his age doesn't matter in a case like this."

He killed people and hurt others, and Garrison may have lifelong problems because of the attack. John Knowles should be sent to prison for the rest of his life.

Sandy listened to her mother's opinion before responding. "Mom, you are going to have to trust me on this. There are reasons he needs to have special treatment that I cannot share with you. I appreciate your concern, but I am doing what is best for Garrison."

"And I am concerned about both you and Garrison! Since George died and you had your last manic episode, I think maybe you haven't been able to think rationally."

"Mom, thank you for caring so much about us, but my psychiatrist, Dr. Robinson and I are watching my situation closely. I'm consulting with him about my decisions and will let him know of your concern."

"Whatever," she answered, "but if I think you are off base, I am going to call your doctor. Remember what happened to you when you were 14."

"Yes, Mom. I remember—I can't forget what happened then. I get it and appreciate that you care. Please trust that I will share with you what I can when I can."

Megan Powell went to the mental health center two days after the attack to examine Dr. Jacob's notes. She was searching for information that could prove John couldn't be held responsible for his violent behavior. While the attorney was reviewing the records, police detectives pursued a thorough criminal investigation to prove John's guilt. They spoke with his teachers, classmates, and neighbors, anyone who may have had an interaction with John that might give a clue as to his mental health status prior to the stabbings.

Seeking further clues as to his recent behavior and any prior incidents of violence, they also interviewed John's maternal grandmother Phyllis, but it was from his mother, Cynthia, they got the all-important backstory.

"Mrs. Knowles," the investigator asked, "did you notice anything different about your son's behavior in the weeks prior to the attack at the school?"

Cynthia searched her memory to recall what she may have seen to help her son. "Come to think of it, he lost his appetite, even for his favorite foods, which was strange. And lately, if I got up during the night, he'd be up, wide awake, pacing, and wringing his hands. When I asked what was bothering him, he just said he was worried about his dad. He said he was angry at God for his dad being injured and deployed all at the same time. I thought that was a normal response to the situation. During the day, he complained about being tired all the time and having daily migraines.

"Then one day," she continued, "he accidentally spilled the dog's food while pouring it into the bowl. Instead of being simply annoyed with himself and cleaning it up, he snatched the bowl and threw it against the wall. That behavior wasn't at all like him. Too, I started getting emails from his teachers saying he fell asleep in class and failed to turn in his assignments. I truly did attribute his actions to being upset because he has ample reason to being so: his dad was wounded in Afghanistan last year and is still recovering at Walter Reed Hospital. Now I know it's more than that. How could I have missed this?"

She paused then, reaching back into her memory for the sad story she needed to tell them. "I know you must think I'm a horrible mother . . . I do." When neither of the detectives responded to the comment, she continued. "I've been too busy commuting back and forth to Walter Reed to visit my husband that I didn't realize my son was sick, too. I should have taken the time to get John evaluated much sooner than I did. I thought it was just stress, but it's so much worse than that." She looked up then with tears flooding her eyes and said, "Detectives, my son has a brain tumor."

Allowing himself a compassionate tone for the distraught woman, Detective Wyatt handed her a box of tissues, "I am sorry to hear this, Ms. Knowles. I know this is all very difficult for you, but please understand, we are just trying to get the facts. Is there anything more you can tell me?"

"Not really. It's hard to think about frankly and even more difficult to talk about," Cynthia said, blowing her nose. "Unless you've been through it you cannot imagine the trauma we're experiencing. I can't bear to think of my son, John, with a ticking time bomb in his brain. He's frightened and sickened by what he's been told he did, but he can't remember any of it. I don't know how to help him and be there for my husband who's lying in a bed in a different city, to say nothing of helping my mom. She has early dementia, and somedays I think I am losing my mind, too."

"Oh, that explains why your mom was very confused when we interviewed her."

"Yes. Sometimes she doesn't know what day it is let alone what happened yesterday. Listen, Detective, I will cooperate in any way I can—I need answers, too, but for now, may I go? I have to pick up my mom's prescriptions before the pharmacy closes."

"Yes, Mrs. Knowles, but stay in touch and keep your phone charged. We will contact you if we need more information."

The next day, John's attorney conducted a separate interview with his mom at their home to extract more details about his conduct in the past few months.

"The last area we have not talked about is how your husband's injury may have impacted John. Do you recall any reaction when you told him about it?"

"Um, no. I tried to be upbeat and spare him the negative horrific details. Of course, he mentioned it, but it seemed he took it okay; he was aware his dad could have died like his friend Garrison's dad did."

"Oh, okay, thank you, Cynthia. That's it for now. I'll be in touch," said Ms. Powell.

When the attorney got into her car, she dialed her former colleague Judge Murphy's backline.

"Henry, It's Megan Powell. How are you coming with that forensic psychiatric order on John Knowles? Because of his fragile medical condition due to advancing cancer, I need it as soon as possible."

"Yes, I finished it not twenty minutes ago," he said. "I gave it to my paralegal and asked that it be faxed immediately. Hold on a minute while I check to see if it went through."

"Thanks for waiting, Megan," he said. "Katie said she faxed it to your office not 10 minutes ago. It should be on your desk as we speak."

"Thank you, Henry," she said. "That's what I was hoping to hear."

"Don't go yet, Megan; you need to hear this," he told her. "Before conferring with the attending physician at Metro, I assigned Dr. Myers, one of the best evaluators we have on staff, to evaluate your client. He's reviewing Dr.

Jacob's notes now to determine whether John is physically stable enough to go through the mental health exam."

"That's a relief to hear, old friend," she told him. "I read the client record too, but if you'll recall, I minored in psychology, but it did nothing to prepare me for something of this complexity. There are so many factors influencing the case: the wounded dad, the demented grandmother, the burned-out mom, and John's own state of mind. Even without a brain tumor, that boy has dealt with enough stress to make anyone blow a gasket."

"I gathered that. It's unfortunate for everyone involved, and there are no easy answers," Judge Murphy said. "Keep me posted, okay, Megan? I need all the details as soon as you get them. Dr. Myers is supposed to do the evaluation at 2pm today, if he thinks young Knowles can handle it."

"Oh, gosh. Thanks for telling me and for everything you're doing, Henry. I'd better go now to be there on time for his evaluation. I want to introduce myself to John before Dr. Myers begins. I will let you know how it goes."

After introducing herself to her new client, Megan Powell sat near the bed and explained what was going to happen next. John, who looked perplexed by everything, mumbled, "Okay, whatever," and turned his face to the wall.

The attorney was silently reviewing her notes when Dr. Myers entered the room. After introducing himself, he turned to John, "Mr. Knowles, I'm Dr. Myers, and I am here to ask you some questions about the incident at the school. Are you willing to cooperate with this process?"

John turned his head to stare at the doctor before saying in a subdued voice, "I will do my best."

"Good," he told him, "Then let's get started. First, can you tell me today's date?"

John, who was puzzled by the question, stumbled on the answer. "Um, is it September? No, that can't be right because I think I have been in school a while. Maybe it's November because there's frost on the window."

The evaluator cleared his throat before proceeding. "Okay, tell me this: do you know the name of the current president?"

The boy scrunched up his face and squeezed his eyes shut. "Well, I know we've had the same guy for a while, but I don't remember his name."

And just like that, Dr. Myers plunged into the reason they were there. "John, do you recall what happened this past Monday morning?"

"Not much," he answered. "I woke up with a pounding headache like the one I have right now," Trying to point to his head with his restrained hands he went on, "It's on the top of my head, and my eyes hurt bad. I remember I was mad that day, but I don't know why." With no warning, John switched gears mid-sentence. Pulling on the handcuffs, he said, "Say, can you explain why I'm wearing handcuffs?"

His eyebrows raised Dr. Myers looked over at the attorney. Dumbfounded by what she'd just heard John say, she just shrugged her shoulders.

The doctor turned back to the boy. "John, you hurt some people."

"I did? Why can't I remember? How are they?" he cried with tears streaming down his face.

Knowing John's actions and their results were discussed during the police interrogation, with the same outcome, Dr. Myers spoke softly, "John, you have a brain tumor, and it's probably affecting your memory. Do you recall Dr. Jacobs telling you about it?"

"No, sir." Then he pulled at the handcuffs again, asking, "Can you tell me why I am in handcuffs? What did I do?"

Glad John couldn't see her, his attorney shook her head and took a deep breath while Dr. Myers prepared to leave to study his findings.

Gently patting the boy on his shoulder, he said, "I think that will be all we need for today."

Just as attorney Powell and the psychiatric evaluator were leaving the room, a nurse came in to take John's vital signs. He turned to her with a vacant stare and asked once more, "Do you know why I am in handcuffs?"

Out of earshot of the guard, the doctor briefly discussed the interview with the attorney. "In all my 20 years of conducting evaluations, I have never interviewed someone so pathetic. I've heard some doozie stories of people trying to fake it, but his body language and words match.

I believe that he does not remember what happened. I don't know if the tumor is fully to blame, but until it is treated, he is not fit to stand trial."

"Thank you, Dr. Myers, that's what I needed to hear," she said. "As soon as you have written your report, please send it to me. I will need to review it before you send it to Judge Murphy."

"Yes, Ma'am, I will have it for you by tomorrow morning."

Based on the results of the "Irresistible Impulse Test" he'd administered, the psychiatrist determined John was mentally incapable of standing trial at that time and that he "did not possess a will sufficient to restrain the impulse that may have arisen from the diseased mind." Too, in an unprecedented move, Dr. Jacobs secured permission for John to start radiation before he was discharged from the hospital. He was then moved to the psychiatric ward at Metro Hospital until he could be transferred to Northern Virginia Mental Health Institute. There, he would be evaluated once again, this time by the Institute's psychiatric staff, to determine if there was improvement in his mental state. The complicating factor was how to get him treatment for the tumor while being confined in the psychiatric ward, necessitating the need for attorney Powell's legal skills. As soon as she got the formal evaluation including the recommendation in hand, she called John's mother.

"Cynthia, this is attorney Powell. If you have a moment, I need to explain where we are with your son's case. It has been determined John is not mentally stable enough to stand trial at this time. This is good news because he needs treatment for his tumor."

"Okay, so what does that mean?" Cynthia responded. "Can you tell me in lay people's terms, please?"

"Of course," she said. "It means I am going to plead with Judge Murphy to issue an order for John to remain in the Metro Psychiatric ward while he receives his cancer treatments. Even though the Metro Psych ward isn't normally equipped to handle long-term patients, I believe if the judge orders it, they will have to accept him."

The attorney heard the joy in Cynthia's voice when she said, "Okay, if you think that will work, then I'm all for it! My son needs help, and this way, we can face the consequences of his actions together."

When the attorney pleaded John's case, Judge Murphy agreed to allow John to remain in the psych ward while he is receiving cancer treatment.

After the decision Judge Murphy said to attorney Powell, " . . .because we are setting a precedent this case will be written up in the law review, but I believe it is warranted. How is the young man, anyway, and how are the surviving victims?"

"Thanks for asking, Henry. It's too soon to determine the long-term physical and psychological effects those kids will have from this incident," she replied with a concerned frown. "And with John getting worse by the day with head pressure and visual disturbances, time is of the essence. Counseling is being offered for anyone who feels the need for it. Frankly, I may need it myself when this is over."

Approaching the open doorway to John's hospital room, Cynthia Knowles glanced briefly at the ever-present guard before walking into her son's room. Receiving a nod in response, she went to the hospital bed where her son lay with his eyes tightly closed. She stood by the bed watching him, loving him, for a few minutes before speaking. "John, it's me—Mom. Can you wake up and tell me how you're doing?"

Rousing, he cracked his eyes open and, in a garbled voice, said, "Oh, hi Mom," followed by a slurred "I love you."

"I love you too, son," she said, gently patting his leg before he fell back asleep.

The guard motioned her time was up. She entered the hallway just as Sandy approached with two cups of steaming coffee. Sandy felt more stable as she continued to see her psychiatrist and consistently took her increased Lamictal medication.

"Hey, girl, I knew you'd be here with your boy and thought you could use this," Sandy said with a smile. "How about we go to the waiting area where you can just sit. You don't have to say a word unless you want to."

By that time, Cynthia was too tired to make decisions, so she followed Sandy without comment. Once settled in the turquoise vinyl seats, her tears began to flow. All too familiar with the stress she was under, Sandy held the two cups until there was a break in the sobbing. Then she handed a cup to Cynthia.

Lifting her bleary eyes to Sandy's, Cynthia said, "I don't know how much more of this I can handle. The doctors at Walter Reed say Joe may be able to come home eventually, but what then? I don't know how to care for his injuries," she said, running her finger around the rim of her cup. "Then there's John. What's going to happen to him?"

"Look, Cynthia, I don't know exactly what you are going through, but I remember how overwhelmed I was when George died. You and others came to my aid then, and I told God I would pay it forward if anyone else ever needed help. So, it's my turn now to help you."

"You *have* helped us, perhaps more than you know," Cynthia told her, "But I am going to need help with John when I return to Walter Reed for a couple of days. If you'd check on my boy while I'm gone, I'd appreciate it. By the way, how is Garrison doing?"

"Thanks for asking about my boy," Sandy told her. "He is gradually improving. He's not back at school—he's still too traumatized to enter the building, but he's receiving therapy at home, which is helping. My mom is at home with him now." When she paused, Cynthia looked up, wondering what was coming next. "Look, I know John would never have done this without the tumor pressing on his brain. I don't blame him."

Holding the cup of coffee close to her chin, Cynthia inhaled its fragrance before saying, "I appreciate what you just said, but I still feel like I failed him as a mother."

Compassion for her friend drove Sandy to act. Putting her cup on the end table, she reached over to hug Cynthia. Crying, they clung to one another until they were 'cried out,' then settled back to discuss the next weeks' schedule and the times Sandy could help with John.

"How about I ask the guard if we can see John for a minute to tell him I will be coming in your absence. He may not remember, but it might help?" Cynthia agreed.

The guard allowed the two women to briefly enter John's room as he stood in the doorway, ready to monitor and to intervene, if necessary. John answered okay sleepily, and Sandy left. Trying to lift his swollen hands from the starched sheets, John slurred, "Mom, I can barely feel my fingers; they feel like sausages."

"I'm sure they do, son. You are on steroids to help with that," she said stroking his brow while tears spilled down her cheeks. "The brain tumor also causes swelling, son. I'm sorry." She left out the part about how the injuries received from others trying to defend themselves and one another added to the swelling.

Witnessing her grief but misunderstanding the cause, he said, "Mom, I am trying to do everything the doctors say, but I can't remember much of anything. Do you know what all those pills they give me are for?"

Trying to keep her son calm, Cynthia took control of her emotions, saying, "When your nurse comes in, we'll ask what each pill is for. Then I'll write it down and tape it to your mirror, so you'll know what you're taking. Will that help?"

Sleepy again, he murmured, "Thanks, Mom."

True to her word, after shift change, Cynthia asked at the nurse's station to speak with the person who would be administering his next medications. Being John's parent, she was allowed to read his chart and communicate with the medical personnel. Nurse Marie was kind and patient. She explained each one before giving it to John, answering Cynthia's questions with the guard observing from the hall. John did not comprehend any of what was said but felt less fearful with his mom present. Cynthia returned the next morning with the typed list.

1. Prednisone is for your swelling.
2. Prevacid is for your heartburn.
3. Lasix is to help remove the extra fluid in your body.
4. Phenobarbital is to control your seizures.

Each time Nurse Marie, Cynthia, or Sandy entered the room they went over the list with John even though he had no understanding of what they were telling him and no remembrance of asking for an explanation of his medications.

As agreed, the next week when Cynthia drove to Walter Reed to be with her husband, Sandy stopped in to see

John. Still too medicated and disoriented to participate in group therapy or anything else, he barely knew she was there, but he seemed more alert. They were all relieved he was transferred to the lockdown ward a week later and no longer required to wear handcuffs.

His attorney, Megan Powell, kept up with her client's progress through regular updates with his mother by phone. In addition, she paid visits to the ward about once a month to document his inability to comprehend the significance of his actions or to stand trial.

Later in the week, when Cynthia was driving back from Walter Reed, she received a call from Dr. Jacobs. "I have spoken with John's oncologist, Dr. Durwood. He would have called you, himself, but he had to perform an emergency surgery this afternoon. He asked me to relay an update. Is that okay?"

"Yes, of course, just let me pull off the road." Safely off the pavement with her flashers on, she said, "Okay, I'm ready."

"Good! Thanks to the radiation he's received, John's tumor has shrunk enough to consider a craniotomy to remove the remainder of it. However, since he continues all the same meds he's been taking, he'll be unable to participate in any kind of psychotherapeutic treatment at this time."

Thinking quickly, Cynthia asked, "When do you think he can have the surgery? Is he strong enough for it?" Before Dr. Jacobs could answer, she added yet another question:

"What are the possible side effects or complications if he has the surgery?"

"Those are excellent questions, Mrs. Knowles, but I'm just the messenger," he told her. "Let me contact Dr. Durwood's office on your behalf to have them arrange a phone consult so you can get those questions answered."

Grateful for his help, she thanked Dr. Jacobs and ended the conversation. Then she sat in the silence of her car for the next twenty minutes sobbing to release the pent-up stress she was holding: feelings of relief for the progress made thus far, the pure exhaustion she felt in every bone of her body, and gut-wrenching fear of what could possibly go wrong. Her cleansing ritual was interrupted by a call from Sandy.

"Hey, girl, are you on the road?" she said brightly. "I figure you're tired and hungry, so are you up for some spaghetti and some vino when you get back in town? I figure you need it. What's your ETA?"

Sniffling, Cynthia thanked her but, instead of going to Sandy's place, suggested, "It's been a long day, and I'm almost too exhausted to hold my head up, but I am starving. Would it be rude of me to ask you to bring dinner to my place? I should be home in about an hour."

"It's no problem to me. Do this," Sandy told her, "Call me on your approach so I can meet you there."

"Sure thing. See you in about an hour."

Later that night, after receiving permission from Cynthia, Sandy called Sam Dawson. "Sam, I talked with Cynthia Knowles just now. She gave me permission to tell you John's doctors have determined the tumor on his brain *is* what caused him to become violent."

The other end of their connection was quiet at first. "Did you hear me, Sam?"

"Yes, yes, I heard you," he responded. "I can't imagine the stress that family has had to endure with Joe's injuries and now this. Tell me, how is Cynthia holding up?"

"I took dinner over there tonight, and we talked for an hour or so," she told him. "I'd say Cynthia is running on fumes. She didn't say it directly, but I suspect she's about to lose her house to say nothing of her mind when you add a husband in the hospital and her son in the lockup ward at the hospital. It's too much for any one person to handle. I want to help, but I don't have the resources either. Luckily, Megan Powell helped me get the benefits I was entitled to when my husband died, or I would have had to do a short sale. I don't have a clue how to navigate all that for Cynthia and her family."

Again, the phone went silent, but not for long. "Hmm, you know what, Sandy? I've got an idea."

"What's that, Sam?"

"I know people at the VA [Veteran's Administration] who can help Cynthia. Do you think she would mind if I checked into it?"

"You have a very kind heart, Sam," she told him. "I should have known you wouldn't want revenge against

John for killing Roger because I know first-hand, you're the best; when my husband died, I would never have gone into therapy without your encouragement."

From the catch in his voice, she knew her words had touched him. "Well, maybe that's what my grief wanted at first, but knowing the circumstances changed my perspective. Maybe it's time to turn my anger into something productive."

"Wow, Sam, that is an answer to prayer. Well, speaking of prayers, it is midnight, and I better say mine and get some shut eye. Tomorrow night, same time?"

"Yup, Sandy, you are my sleepy-time tonic," he told her in the deep gravelly voice she'd come to enjoy. "Thanks, and good night."

"Good night, Sam," she told him. "Sleep tight and don't let the bedbugs bite, or the nightmares getcha."

"You are one funny woman, Sandy Jones. G'night," he said softly.

Not a man to waste time, Sam set up a GoFundMe page for Cynthia before retiring that night, seeding the fledgling fund with his own money as an anonymous donor.

Sandy arranged for Sam to meet with Cynthia the following day to tell her about his offer to use his contacts with the VA on her behalf. Cynthia was astounded. Considering her son killed Sam's son, his compassion and generosity, were hard to accept at first. "Thanks Sam. I knew you were a good man, but after Sandy told me how you helped her, and now offering to help my family, I know now you're more than good; you might just be an angel."

Sam knew he was not an angel, but he *was* a retired veteran. As such, he knew to call the Veteran's Disability Benefit Services Department at the VA about benefits for Wounded Warriors.

"Hello, this is Sgt. Samuel Dawson retired. I'm calling to see what resources are available to cover the living expenses and other needs of the Knowles family." He then proceeded to present the tragic details."

The results of his inquiries at the VA went beyond helping Cynthia catch up on her delinquent mortgage payments; funding was also provided to cover the cost of adapting their house so Joe could eventually come home.

When Sam informed Cynthia of the call, she said, "Thanks does not fully express my gratitude for what you have done to help my family and me. I know hope for the first time since this nightmare began."

One night, after his nightly call with Sandy, Sam was restless and couldn't sleep. Turning to the television for distraction, he discovered serendipity at play: it was an interview with Kate Grosmaire, author of *Forgiving my Daughter's Killer.* In it, Grosmaire used a term new to him: Restorative Justice, which he learned has been around since the 1970s and is about repairing multi-faceted damage caused by a perpetrator. He immediately looked up her book on Amazon and read the description "Kate Grosmaire tells the story of her daughter's murder at the hand of her boyfriend—and the stunning, deliberate forgiveness and help that Kate and her husband offered to the young man who shattered their world." He knew he had to have a copy so, he downloaded the Kindle version and began reading.

Excited and motivated, the next night, Sam told Sandy what he'd learned so far about Restorative Justice during their evening FaceTime visit. "Sandy, what would you think about suggesting this for John?"

"I just don't know, Sam," she said with a hint of caution in her voice. "This isn't up to you and me to decide. I will bring it up with John's attorney and Cynthia if you want. Do you have any materials I can share with them?"

"Sure, I Googled a bunch and can send the links over in a few minutes. I just need to fire up my computer."

"Thanks, I'll let you know what Ms. Powell and Cynthia say."

With support from Cynthia, Sandy, and attorney Powell, Sam shared the concept of Restorative Justice with families from the school tragedy and its potential for their community. In addition, he joined online groups and researched other communities who had developed similar programs; consequently, deciding to spearhead a local project to promote healing for both John and his victims.

A Year After the Incident

JOHN'S SURGERY WAS completed 53 weeks after the school incident. Cynthia prayed the surgery would be successful. Because her husband was in rehab on an extensive physical therapy regimen, she was not needed as much at Walter Reed and could help John with his rehab.

Two weeks postop, she received an answer to her prayer. "Hey, Mom, look at this!" John said as he gingerly eased his body out of the bed and walked haltingly, holding on to the bedrail to the bathroom door. "What was it you told me yesterday about my dad?"

Tears trickled down Cynthia's nose. "You remembered something. That's fantastic!"

"Well, I remembered you told me something, but I don't remember what it was."

"I said Dad has moved from the wheelchair to a walker. So maybe you two can eventually see each other in person."

"Oh, yeah. Maybe we could FaceTime until then."

"I will check with your attorney to see if that is allowed and with the staff to see how and where to do that. You would hardly recognize each other. It has been almost two years since you were with each other."

John got quiet and Cynthia observed his change in demeanor. He looked up at his mom and asked, "Did I really kill people? I can't believe it. I want it to be a bad dream. I keep thinking I should have been the one to die, not them. Maybe those families would be better off if I was dead."

"Son, don't say that, you were not in your right mind. The brain tumor is the cause, not you, so get that thought out of your head. Besides, I need you to live and for you, your dad, and me to be a family again, all living in the same house. That means you, me, and your dad. "

"Mom, that may never happen. I could be sent away for the rest of my life," John said with tears welling up.

Surprised that her son had such dark thoughts Cynthia changed the topic to something more pleasant. As soon as her allotted visiting time was over, she called his treating physician. "Dr. Jacobs, I am pleased that John has some memory back, but I am now concerned that the memories are affecting his desire to live."

"How so, Mrs. Knowles? Did he say something to make you think that?"

"Sort of. He thinks the families he harmed would be better off if he were dead. I know he doesn't have any means to kill himself, but I worry with that attitude he

A Year After the Incident | 73

might refuse treatment that could prevent the cancer from returning."

"I see. Yes, that is common when someone has gone through what he has. When I make my rounds, I will discuss it with him and see what he needs. I may add an anti-depressant to his regimen and put him on suicide watch."

"Thank you, Dr. Jacobs for all you have and are doing for my son."

"Glad I can help Mrs. Knowles. We will do what we can for John."

After a conversation with John, Dr. Jacobs added an antidepressant medication and put the staff on high alert concerning his suicidal thinking.

When Attorney Powell would be coming for her monthly visit, Cynthia would write a reminder on the erasable whiteboard. Four weeks after surgery when the attorney came for her regular visit, she found John more cognitively aware. "Hello, John, how are you feeling?

"My mom says I am remembering some things."

"Is that good or bad for you, John?" the attorney inquired in her best compassionate voice.

"Some things are okay, like remembering my fifth birthday party and my dad at home before he went on his last deployment. But what I don't remember is what I did at school that day," John said with a blank stare.

"Oh, I see," said attorney Powell. "As you remember more, then you may have questions, but I am not sure I can be the one to answer them. However, at some point we must discuss what happens for your future concerning that day. I don't think you are ready for that discussion today, but how about we discuss it on my next monthly visit?"

"Yes, Ma'am. I will if I can."

"Good, until next month then." She said as she shook his hand, then went to her car and cried. *How can this young man ever redeem himself? Will the tumor come back and cause him to be violent again? How should I advise him? Would the insanity plea hold up? I will wait until he is more cognitively aware to understand the charges and then advise him. I'm glad I have another month before I must figure this out.*

When Megan Powell returned the next month, she had knots in her stomach. How would she find John? After a brief conversation about his progress, she broached the subject, sensing he was ready to begin the process.

"John, are you ready to discuss your future?"

"Do you mean whether I will spend the rest of my life in prison or not?" he said with eyes downcast.

Knowing she must take a harder line with the frightened teenager; she took a different approach. "John Knowles, look at me. Do you want me to be honest with you?"

Reluctantly making eye contact with his attorney, the boy responded in a sad voice. "I guess so, but I don't know if I can handle what you tell me or remember what you say."

Her own heart constricting at his words, she responded in a softer voice. "That's understandable, so let's put it this way: you have some options. The prosecution could either request you be tried as an adult, or you could be sent to a youth correctional prison until you are an adult. Another option is you could be acquitted because of the brain tumor which caused you to act out in anger, or you might be released on probation for a specified length of time."

"What does acquitted mean?"

"It means you could be found not guilty because you were not in your right mind at the time of the crime."

"You mean when I killed those people?"

"Technically, yes, but knowing your history, I believe without that brain tumor, you would have never committed those crimes. So, I want you to think about all this and let me know how you want me to proceed."

Looking her straight in the eye, he said, "Do I have to tell you right now? Cause if I do, I'd have to say lock me away and throw away the key."

Attorney Powell knew that was an impulsive answer that she did not accept. I will come back next week, and we can discuss it further. I will talk to your mom and tell her what I have shared with you, okay?"

John's attorney left him with a troubled expression on his young face. *He needs his mom right now*, she thought and pulled over to phone Cynthia.

When Sandy came to visit the next afternoon, John wanted to discuss his future with her. She, however, was concerned about the legalities of discussing his case without his attorney being present.

"John, your future is an important topic, and I'm honored you'd trust me to talk with you about it, but let's wait until either your mom or attorney is here when we do. Are you all right with that?"

John, who knew nothing about the legalities involved, reluctantly agreed to speak with the attorney and his mom first but insisted he needed to speak with Ms. Sandy, too. She was a trusted resource perfect for his needs, and one who provided an outside opinion apart from that of his mom who was overwrought with worry about him and his dad.

On the day of Sandy's scheduled visit with John, he was sitting in a wheelchair staring out the window. She opened the door, and attorney Powell walked in behind her. "Hey, John, look who came with me today. Is this a good time to discuss your future?"

The shadow of a smile creased his young face when he saw them. "Sure! My future is all I can think about right now. Thank you both for coming."

They sat in the corner of the visitors' room, away from other patients to speak privately. Pushing the niceties aside after that, his attorney was all business. She unfolded a detailed spreadsheet out on a side table of all John's possible options for his consideration.

After discussing several of his options, Sandy interrupted the discussion to expedite the final topic on the list—Restorative Justice.

"What's that?" John inquired.

"You know John, my neighbor, Mr. Dawson, well, he heard an interview about it on television as an option for cases like yours." Then she turned to the attorney, "Can you inform us if Restorative Justice is a possibility for John?"

"Of course! I'm just surprised I didn't think of it before you suggested it a couple of weeks ago. It is a process whereby the person who committed a crime recognizes the need to repair the damage they did to individuals and their families. It involves reparation or taking action to repair the injury perpetrated. It might just work in your case, John. Let me look into it more, and then I'll discuss it with you and your mom, okay?"

Before she could say any more, Sandy interrupted. "They already know about it. I've already sent the Restorative Justice information Mr. Dawson collected to your mom and the families of the victims. I will bring you some too, if you want, John."

"Okay, thank you, Ms. Sandy."

When the two women left his room, John prayed, *God, if this could help some of the people I hurt, please let it, no matter what happens to me.*

Community Recovery

FIFTEEN MONTHS AFTER the school stabbings, Cynthia's worry lines were permanently etched in her face. The grey in her hair matched her complexion. She had lost twenty pounds and slept maybe five hours on a good night. She alternated her time between visiting her brain-injured husband now in rehab at Walter Reed and helping her son recover from brain surgery and the effects of radiation on his body while he continued to be detained in Metro Psych ward. She navigated all the legal red tape to get what her son and husband needed. Joe could not comprehend what day it was, let alone understand how his son could be capable of such an act, so she chose not to tell him or initiate FaceTime calls between him and John. The Walter Reed medical personnel knew the circumstances but kept it confidential.

Though her own son Garrison had largely recovered from his wounds and was now released from treatment, Sandy continued to visit John, whose mom was still making weekly trips to the Veteran's Hospital.

John's progress was impressive. He was consistent with his exercises, his gait was stronger, and when he stood up, he was steadier on his feet for short periods.

A Nurse Practitioner in the Psychiatric Unit approached Sandy one day while she was visiting him. "Ms. Jones, our patient here talks about you frequently, so I decided it was time to meet you! I'm Clare, a nurse practitioner assigned to this unit. I've heard you are helping John while his mom is tending to his father at Walter Reed."

"Hello, it's good to meet you," Sandy said, extending her hand. "Yes, I help John with his rehab exercises when Cynthia can't be here, but I'm no saint. So, unfortunately, I can only come after work a couple of times a week."

While John continued working on his exercises, Sandy and the nurse practitioner talked nearby. "We really appreciate your help," Clare said. "Our staff's time is limited to mental health tasks, and unfortunately, the physical therapist only comes to this unit three times a week."

"Certainly. I am glad to help when and where I can, but it's a form of payback for me; people helped me after a roadside bomb killed my husband, so now I'm returning the favor."

Clare's kind face immediately showed concern. "I'm so sorry for your loss, Mrs. Jones. That must have been hard for you."

"Yes, and it was complicated by my own mental illness. But, thanks to the support of this community, I was able to bounce back. Without their help, I'm sure

I would never have made it. That's why it's important to me that John and his family have the same opportunities I was given."

"Good for you. If there is something you need to help this young man, let us know.

We have grown to love him and to treat him like our own."

Turning back to the bed, Sandy saw John, who'd heard bits of their conversation, smile for the first time in weeks.

With the approval of John's attorney, Megan Powell, Cynthia, and Sam proceeded to research the tenets of Restorative Justice and how they could best be applied to John's case. Using that information, they formed a task force called "Restorative Justice Recovery Project (RJRP).

The initial task force consisted of the parents of the victims, victim-survivors, Police Chief Daniels, Judge Murphy, Chaplain Curtis, Dr. Myers, Dr. Rodriquez, Dr. Jacobs, and anyone else who would listen and cared to participate.

"Sam," Sandy said in a late-night phone chat. "I'm so proud of you for spearheading this project. I know Roger is proud of you too."

Though she couldn't see them, Sandy knew by the tone of his voice Sam's eyes were glistening with tears. She knew, too, he had stopped trying to hold back what he felt when she heard his next words. "I could not have done this without you, Sandy."

Inspired by the legal intricacies of the John Knowles case, the core RJ (Restorative Justice) committee created a template to use both with his and future cases. The initial action plan included the following:

- A listening conference to allow surviving victims and deceased victims' families to meet with the perpetrator in person to begin a dialogue about what they needed to begin to heal.
- They set April 13 as the beginning date for the conference and reserved the meeting room just outside the hospital's psychiatric ward.
- It was agreed John would be handcuffed during the session and accompanied by a hospital security officer. This officer would remain in the room the entire time.
- John's in-patient mental health therapist would also be present and would stop proceedings if she felt the discussion was damaging to anyone attending the meeting.

Though the plan was approved unanimously, Sandy, anxious about how things would go, made sure she took her Lamictal on time before the group gathered on April 13th to meet with John. The frail young man wearing gray sweats entered the room in a wheelchair, obviously frightened. As the security guard assisted transferring him into the upholstered chair at the head of the table, everyone could see John's unsteady body swaying. Though he was clearly not the robust, scary person they imagined him to be, this was the kid whose actions changed their lives forever.

Yvonne Lynch almost bolted out of the room, afraid that the butterflies in her stomach would cause her to vomit. Instead, she settled as she prayed the Serenity Prayer. John's mom decided upon the advice of attorney Powell not to attend the meeting. She was not emotionally prepared to handle all that the victims and families may sling at her son. She preferred to support John afterward.

Sensing an emotional charge in the room, Sandy serving as the moderator for the first session, broke the silence. "John, it is good to see you. How are you?"

Hearing her familiar voice, he looked up with the ghost of a smile. "It's good to see you too, Ms. Sandy— I'm glad you're here. My doctors say I'm getting better, though my progress is slow."

"I'm glad to hear it," she told him with a gentle smile. "We are here to begin healing the community using a process called Restorative Justice. Judge Murphy, the prosecutor, Attorney Megan, and these parents have all approved the method. Now, some of the parents of the victims are going to ask you some questions and tell you how they feel." She paused then to look him in the eye before asking, "Are you ready for this?"

Staring at his thin, handcuffed hands folded on the table, he said, "I don't know if I can, but I will try."

Sandy said, "That is all we ask. Okay, let's begin. First, Sam, identify yourself for John, then state your first question for him."

"Yes. John, I am Roger's father, Sam Dawson. He was my only child—my son. He died from a stab wound you inflicted upon him. Do you know why I came?"

Unsure how to respond to the question at first, John stared in silence at Sam, his face pale. "No, sir, I do not, but I guess you want to yell at me for what I did to Roger. I bet you want me to spend the rest of my life in prison."

"To be honest, John, maybe I did at first, but not now. Please just listen to the others, okay?"

John answered respectfully, "Yes, sir."

At Sam's nod, Anita Nelson spoke next. Her voice, normally strong and forceful, was soft. "John, I'm Tim's mom, Anita Nelson. You stabbed my son in the chest that day at the school. He survived, but our family is still deeply hurt and scarred by what you did. But no, John, I don't want you locked up forever. Seeing that scar on the top of your head, I can tell you've been through quite an ordeal, too, but it doesn't explain why you put that knife in my boy. Still, I am willing to work through it with you."

John let out a sigh of relief and looked up at Tim's mom as tears trickled down his cheeks and mucus poured from his nose. "I am so sorry about what I did to Tim, but I can't remember what happened, and I have tried. Dr. Jacobs says it may be because it is too painful to remember, so my brain has blocked it. If I could bring back the people I hurt, I would."

Officer Patterson spoke next. "John, I am Monique Patterson's uncle. You killed my niece when she tried to help Mr. Hughes. You didn't just hurt a couple of people; you killed three and caused injuries to another four, not counting the emotional trauma for their families and all those who witnessed what you did. There is nothing you can do to bring them back—it's an empty place we can never fill. You may say you're sorry, and that may be true, but you must be punished for what you did."

Sandy interrupted him at that point. "Officer Patterson, we know you mean well, but those words will not help us all heal. I have known John since he was nine years old, so I know that before the tumor he would not have hurt a fly. No one here denies he committed a terrible crime that day, but he lost something, too: the tumor stole his ability to reason or to know right from wrong."

Wanda, John's counselor, stood up and said, "I must remind you this is a listening conference, so let's keep it going in a positive direction. Otherwise, I will stop the process. If John gets upset, it may cause a setback in his recovery, and that will benefit no one."

Unable to continue due to his conflicting emotions, Officer Patterson stood and spoke to the group. "Please, everyone, excuse me. I can't handle any more today." Taking his ravaged feelings with him, he left the room. Though the tension subsided at his departure, they were all reminded of what the cost of John's crime meant to each one.

Sandy suggested a ten-minute restroom break during which the group members scattered. At first, she worried they might not return, but in precisely ten minutes, they reassembled, ready to proceed.

Sandy nodded for Sam to begin. With a solemn expression, he turned to John, "Young man, I hope you have some understanding of the emotional stress these people are experiencing by coming here, but relieving that pressure is part of why we are in this room with you. The way you can help us is called Restorative Justice—if you'll recall, you were told about it a couple of weeks ago . . ." Seeing John's blank expression told Sam the concept would need more explanation if it were to work. "That's okay, John, we'll explain it to you. We call it RJ, and it's a way you can help us deal with the loss of our children at your hand. Are you willing to hear about it?"

"Yes, sir. Mr. Dawson. I am."

"Folks, pull out this handout from your folder," the grieving father said, holding up his copy of the article from www.TPRonline.org written by Sandra Pavelka O'Brien, Ph.D. called *Restorative Justice: Principles, Practices, and Application.* He began reading it out loud to make certain all understood what was involved.

"The reason we are here today John is spelled out in the 4th aspect of the Victim's section, which states that victims have the opportunity to face the offender and tell their story to the offender and others if they so desire. That is why we are telling you about our pain and asking you questions. Do you understand this, John?"

"Not totally, sir, but I am trying."

"Okay, son. We will guide you along the process.

"The next step is when your oncologist and surgeon say you are ready, you and I will begin visiting school assemblies in this area to speak about the cause and result of your actions that day at the school. A law officer will accompany us because you are still technically in their custody. Our goal in doing this is to help others who may also have violent tendencies, whether medically induced or not. The hope is when they hear your story, troubled students will know they're not alone, that help is available, and maybe your speaking will prevent future tragedies. Are you interested in helping those kids, John? Keep in mind depending on how you perform this community service may positively influence the outcome of a trial or a plea."

"Mr. Dawson, and all of you in this room, I want to do what I can to help, but right now, I'm still having seizures, and I'm not very steady on my feet. I can't remember what happened that day beyond my head hurting and that I felt angry. How can I tell my story if I don't remember it?"

Sandy, seeing he was confused, spoke up. "John, there are written witnesses' accounts of the attack which can help you reconstruct the chain of events. You won't have to prepare by yourself—your therapist Wanda will help you write and practice it."

John's therapist nodded in agreement. "That I will, Mrs. Jones, but Dr. Jacobs will be a part of our team, too." She turned to John and said, "With Dr. Jacobs' and everyone's help, you will work your way through this, but only at a pace you can handle emotionally. What do you think so far?"

"I guess I can if you all help me." John responded but there was a note of concern in his voice. "I just can't do it alone. What if I get angry again? Then what?"

Wanda spoke up. "John, I understand your concern about losing control, but the tumor that caused your behavior has now been removed and you are taking medication to prevent behavior like that again. So long as you consistently take your medication to prevent your tumor from returning and other meds, you're unlikely to experience violence again. We will make certain you take your medications on time, and your oncologist, Dr. Durwood, and your psychiatrist, Dr. Jacobs will have an on-going say if they think it is safe to do this Restorative process. Okay?"

John shook his head affirmatively and his shoulders relaxed. Then he slumped in the chair, too exhausted for any more conversation. Wanda feared the process had overwhelmed him and caused a physical set back. She knew it was all he could handle for one day. She stood up and said it was time for him to return to the unit for his afternoon meds. She followed the security guard as he wheeled John out of the room.

The group of grieving parents and professionals spoke briefly among themselves. "I didn't realize John was so ill, but I see it now. Seeing him for myself has helped calm my emotions; I'm not nearly as angry with him as I was," said Carmen's mother.

When officer Patterson returned to the room, he said, "folks, I'm sorry for my outburst of anger. I just got back from my sister's place in Kansas where I have been for the last year. I had blocked out the trauma. I don't know what I expected to feel when I came back here, but I've discovered I'm still angry and lost. I can't just snap out of it."

Sam put his arm around him saying, "I know, brother. There isn't a moment that goes by that I don't wish this were just a horrific nightmare and I will wake up." All the room nodded in agreement.

Sandy spoke up, "Officer Patterson, I had to see a therapist to deal with my trauma. It helped. There is a victim fund that can help cover the cost. Let me know if you want the information."

"Okay, let me think about it," he said, more composed. Sandy handed him a brochure as he was exiting the room. He stuck it in his jacket pocket.

Three months after their first meeting, the RJ Task Force gathered again, this time to determine the next move on their outlined schedule—that of getting John to tell his story to a group of middle school students. Their local district decided the community's emotions were still too raw to have it there, so neighboring Fairfax County invited him to speak to their mid-grade students.

When John arrived in the County transport van, he emerged looking like any other sweats-clad disabled student, except he was pushed in his wheelchair by an off-duty police officer to the assembly hall.

He almost panicked when there was no sign of Sam Dawson. Not until he and the guard were settled backstage waiting for the principal to call him out did John see the man who gave him fleeting hope. Sam's welcoming smile when he entered from the side door ramp reassured him; if Mr. Dawson could do this with the kid who killed his son, then he, the boy who did it, would do everything in his power to work with him and try and help others. At John's surprise on seeing him, Sam shook his hand, saying, "I promised you I'd be here, didn't I? I keep my promises, son." That comment caused tears to well up in John's eyes, so he added, "I believe you can do this, John. These kids need to hear your story so tell it straight from your heart. Principal Edwards asked me to go first. I will explain a bit about what happened that day and why we chose to employ the principles of Restorative Justice to help us all deal with our emotions and begin healing. Then I'll introduce you. Ah—that's my call," he said, patting the boy's shoulder. Then he went through the curtains and onto the stage to address the students.

Despite the fear he felt about telling his own story about what he could remember from that horrible day, John was mesmerized by Sam Dawson's presentation, as were the students. They hung on his every word, trying to imagine what Dawson felt on hearing his only son was dead and that he, John Knowles, who was just a normal kid until then, was his killer.

When the guard pushed John's chair to center stage, the gym fell silent. He looked so small and insignificant up there, but it soon became clear nothing about him, or his story was insignificant. His former Principal, Mr. Edwards—the educator who transferred to this school to escape the daily reminders of what happened that day, introduced him. Mr. Edwards' hands were shaking when he gave John the mic.

When it was time for their contemporary to speak, everyone saw the fear on his face and in his voice; his hand shook so badly he could barely take the mic when the principal solemnly handed it to him. Fortunately, Sam kept his promise, standing next to the wheelchair with his hand on John's shoulder until he could get his nerves under control.

Nineteen months earlier, when students heard the news about the stabbings through various media outlets including features on national television, they were shocked. Now, their faces simultaneously registered curiosity about the frail boy on stage and horror at what he had done. It was apparent they could hardly believe he was sitting in a wheelchair in their gym telling them about it.

Haltingly, his voice thin and raspy, John told them what he could remember from that day. He held nothing back, telling them about his sudden unexplainable anger, the pain, horror, sorrow, and regret he experienced both then and now. It was a story none of them would ever forget, and it was one he forced out between heart-wrenching sobs. No one heckled him; even the tough kids listened.

When John finished telling his story, there was dead silence except for the weeping heard amongst some affected students. Then when one tough kid stood up on the bleachers; Mr. Edwards' blood pressure immediately shot up, fearing he might create a scene. Instead, a rough kid from an underprivileged neighborhood started to clap. Caught off guard, the fellow students turned to look at him not responding at first, but then they all stood up, clapped, and cheered. Sam and John looked at one another and, with tears streaming down their cheeks, hugged each other. With the crowd being managed by the teachers, students lined up to shake John's and Mr. Dawson's hand. Afterward the students were directed to a sign-up table where they could register to become part of a school movement to quell violence called TS (Tell Someone).

Word about Restorative Justice spread rapidly in the community after that, with the court system experiencing an outpouring of victims wanting to help their attackers.

Soon, Restorative Justice became a buzzword in the community embraced by many.

John, who grew more comfortable sharing his story the more often he told it, began to remember it in greater detail in future talks. Fortunately for him, his RJ mentors, and especially his therapist, were there to help him work through the additional traumas he encountered with the return of those memories. He also grew closer to Sam Dawson, whose sad eyes emanated trustworthiness and compassion both for him and for others. As a result, with Judge Murphy's consent, Dr. Jacobs allowed Sam to meet regularly with John to plan for upcoming appearances.

When the Rehabilitation Unit at Walter Reed notified Cynthia Knowles, preparing to release her husband Joe to her care, the community responded with offers to construct a sturdy ramp and a handicap accessible addition to the Knowles' home. The Veteran's Administration Wounded Warrior Project would provide the funding. Though he still needed assistance to recover from the traumatic brain injury, having her husband at home eased the burden on Cynthia. Joe, having been informed, supports what must be done.

Epilogue

TWO YEARS FROM the first evaluation, Dr. Jacobs said John was ready for a second evaluation. Afterwards, Dr. Meyers, the forensic psychiatrist, determined John was competent to understand what he did and to have his day in court. Based on the strategizing with the RJRP task force, it was decided it was in the best interest of everyone affected by John's actions that he stays the next two years until he turns 18 at the Youth Correctional Facility. As part of his sentence, he would continue to speak around the area. Once completed he would have no parole. He wrote an apology to each surviving victim and deceased victim's family, vowing to continue the speaking engagements after serving his sentence. The Metro Psych ward, normally a short-term treatment facility made an exception based on Judge Murphy's ruling to allow John to remain there for the length of his recovery prior to his sentencing. He had become a permanent fixture in the ward, helping other patients adjust to the routine and be compliant with their doctor's orders. The day he was transported to the Youth Correctional facility, many staff members wept.

Speaking of promises, Sandy Jones kept the one she made to Sam Dawson: she is there for him. She answers when he needs to talk though now their conversations are frequently based on the progress of RJRP.

Officer Patterson finally forgave John after intense trauma psychotherapy, but he decided to leave town and build a new life in Kansas near his sister.

Each injured student had treatment using a specific method called Eye Movement Desensitization and Reprocessing (EMDR) therapy. It is a tool designed to lessen the trauma effect on the person's mind and body so they can think about the event without being re-traumatized. It involves waving a wand with a light on it in front of the client's eyes. They also were taught anxiety-lessening techniques to help resolve their diagnosis of Post-Traumatic Stress Disorder.

Once John was officially incarcerated, the detention center allowed Sam Dawson to volunteer to tutor John so he could graduate on time with his peers. Sam will also assist in transitioning him back into society, where he will continue to tell his story; he and Sam are collaborating on writing a book about their experience with Restorative Justice.

John in turn has tutored fellow inmates to lower the recidivism rate the lack of education causes. He has also befriended those who lack the family support he is lucky to have. John will be released in June on his 18th birthday. His cancer continues to be in remission.

After Garrison Jones graduated from high school in May with plans to enter the Citadel in the fall, his mom decided to try dating again—with her son's approval and a likely candidate in mind.

After she and Sam discussed moving their friendship to the next level, that same evening he issued an invitation, "Hey, Sandy. What do you say we go out for a cup of coffee tomorrow night instead of our late-night phone chat?"

"Sure, Sam, that would be nice just so long as it's not a lukewarm macchiato."

Discussion Questions

QUESTIONS FOR SCHOOLS, Churches, Businesses, and Civic Groups

1. Have you or someone you know been a victim of a crime?
2. How did that crime impact your/their life?
3. Have you intentionally or unintentionally harmed someone either physically, mentally, emotionally, financially, or socially?
4. If so, how do you look at that situation now?
5. Have you tried to make amends to the people you harmed?
6. Has anyone you harmed tried to communicate with you?
7. What was your response?
8. Do you know someone who is inflicting or planning to inflict harm on someone?
9. Have you tried listening to that person and offering options to help lessen their anger?

10. What methods can you use to lessen your anger about situations? If you feel someone could potentially harm you, how can you protect yourself?
11. With whom do you discuss your fears and feelings?
12. Do you believe someone, or something could have averted John's violence? If so, what, and how?

The Effects of Trauma on Mental Health

1. Do you believe Sandy's bipolar mania is a product of genes, environment, or both?
2. When she was out of control trying to orchestrate the crisis, could you see what was happening inside her mind?
3. Have you ever felt like Sandy?
4. What is your opinion about Sandy's psychiatrist and colleagues orchestrating behind the scenes to keep her stable and from inflicting harm in the situation?
5. Do you think Sandy was out of line trying to help John?
6. Can you think of a different method that could have helped?
7. Do you think Meg was right to tell Sandy she was worried about her since she was not sure she could support Sandy through this new emotional roller coaster?

8. Do you think Sam is wise entertaining the idea of starting a relationship with Sandy, a manic, medically controlled woman?

Action

1. Does your school/place of employment have a program for students/employees to report or help someone who feels left out, bullied, or unheard?
2. Are you willing to start or support such a project?
3. How could you employ Restorative Justice in your family, church, school, office?
4. Is there someone you know who needs therapy to recover from trauma, and would you be willing to speak up about it and to attend the first session with them?
5. Discuss with your group how you have recovered from trauma.

Table 5.1[1]
Restorative Justice: Three-Dimensional Collaboration

VICTIMS

- Receive support, assistance, compensation, information, and services.
- Receive restitution and/or other reparation from the offender.
- Are involved and encouraged to provide input at all points in the justice process, including direct input into how the offender will repair the harm done.
- Has an opportunity to face the offenders and tell their story to offenders and others, if they so desire.
- Feel satisfied with the justice process.

Adopted from: *O'Brien and Bozemore, 2005.* Table Reprint granted October 15, 2021, by Sandra Pavelka O'Brien by email.

- Provide guidance and consultation to professionals on planning and advisory groups.

OFFENDERS

- Complete restitution to their victims.
- Provide meaningful service to repay the debt to their communities.
- Face the personal harm caused by their crimes by participating in victim offender mediation, if the victim is willing, or through other victim awareness processes.
- Complete work experience and tasks which increase skills and improve the community.
- Monitored by community adults as well as justice providers and supervised to the greatest extent possible in the community.
- Improve decision-making skills and have opportunities to help others.

FAMILIES AND COMMUNITY MEMBERS

- Are involved to the greatest extent possible in offender accountability and rehabilitation, and in developing community safety initiatives.
- Work with offenders on local community service projects.
- Provide support to victims.
- Provide work for offenders so they can pay restitution to victims.

- Provide service opportunities that allow offenders to learn skills and make meaningful contributions to the quality of community life.
- Assist families to support young offenders in their obligation to repair the harm and increase competencies.
- Play an advisory role to courts and corrections and/or play an active role in disposition through one or more neighborhood sanctioning process.
- Act as mentors to assist offenders with developing competencies, including completing job applications, studying for GED or school tests, and becoming productive members of society.

Resources

Center for the Prevention of School Violence: 1-800-299-6504

Circles documentary by Cassidy Friedman—https://cssj.org/ we-are-survivors/ (Crime Survivors of Safety and Justice)

Forgiving my Daughter's Killer by Kate Grosmaire

National Association of Community and Restorative Justice — https://nacrj.org/

O'Brien-Pavelka, S. (December 2007). Restorative Justice: Principles, Practices, and Application. *The Preventative Researcher,* Volume 14. Retrieved October 6, 2021 from www.TPRonline.org

Wildflowers in the Median: A Restorative Journey into Healing, Justice, and Joy by Furey and Leonard Scovens

https://www.restorativeresources.org/educator-toolkit.html

Restorative Justice for schools—https://www.edutopia.org/ blog/restorative-justice-resources-matt-davis

About the Author

MELANIE BARTON BRAGG has a master's degree in social work, a doctorate in pastoral counseling and community development, and is an ordained Christian Church (Disciples of Christ) minister with Ecclesiastical Endorsement as a pastoral counselor. Since 1985 Dr. Barton Bragg has maintained a private holistic psychotherapy practice. She is a Reiki and Rife practitioner. Her work has included teaching at the college level, leading multiple workshops, and consulting with organizations and churches to navigate through transitions, including educating them about sexual addiction. As a trained crisis responder, Dr. Barton debriefs critical incidents in private and governmental agencies.

Archived episodes of her two-and-a-half-year Internet radio show are available for listening to on her website www.thedrmelanieshow.com. She has been interviewed on television, radio, and online live events. Her three published books are The ABCs of Children's Sermons, Quicksand: Marion's Memories Married to a Sex Addict Minister, Clergy Sexual Misconduct: A Layperson's Guide to Predict, Prevent, Detect,

Address, Treat, and Recover from Clerical Sexual Abuse all available on Amazon. She enjoys living in North Florida and spending time with her children and grandchildren. To contact her to lead your workshop, seminar, webinar, or teleconference, or to become a virtual client contact her at drmelaniebarton@gmail.com.

Create a MOVEMENT in your community to PREVENT school and workplace VIOLENCE.

Learn how victims of critical incidences and assailants can heal using RESTORATIVE JUSTICE methods.

Visit www.TheDrMelanieShow.com

Additional Works

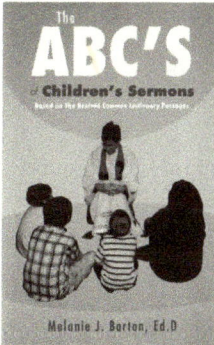

Children's sermons are often inadequately prepared, understood maybe only by the adults, and leave the youth wanting something to which they can relate.

Because children take what you say literally, the stories need to be brief, to the point, and use simple and age-appropriate words. Leaders need to get and stay on the children's eye level.

ISBN: 9781449768577
$17.95 | 224 pgs
ASIN: B0792WBGTQ
$3.99

This book will help you do that by offering a written sample story related to one of the weeks lectionary passages. An accompanying auditory example is told on the CDs. Each lesson tells you what props are needed. The storyteller is encouraged to include some of their own personal walk with God to make the sermonettes come alive. These tools will prepare you to plan ahead to present a relevant, effective message that the boys and girls will not only learn from but will come back wanting to hear more.

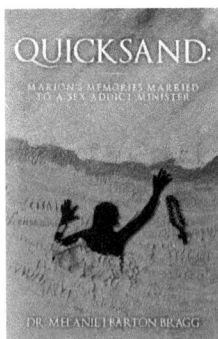

On a journey from suffering to salvation, one woman finds the inner strength to overcome her abusive past and painful present to emerge from the quicksand and face a future filled with joy.

Then comes the cancer diagnosis. But Marion has finally decided that enough is enough, so she embarks on a path of healing. Through breakthroughs in psychotherapy, she finds that she can look past her harrowing experiences, break the chains that bind her to misery, and move toward a new life of wholeness — and freedom.

ISBN: 9781979449182
$18.38 | 469 pgs
ASIN: B078JQ728Q
$2.99

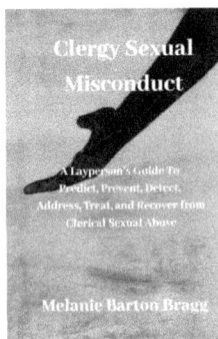

When stress, isolation, and a history of family dysfunction accompany a minister into their calling, it can lead a person to disaster unless preemptively addressed.

People of the pews need to be educated to prevent, predict, discover, address, treat, and recover from the effects of clergy sexual abuse /misconduct /addiction. This guide will do that.

ISBN: 9798605712343
$15 | 114 pgs
ASIN: B084HLLLYK
$2.99

www.ingramcontent.com/pod-product-compliance
Lightning Source LLC
Chambersburg PA
CBHW031520270326
41930CB00006B/450